INTERNATIONAL LABOUR
LEGISLATION

Navigia atque agri culturas moenia leges

* * * *

usus et impigrae simul experientia mentis
paulatim docuit pedetentim progredientis.
Sic unum quicquid paulatim protrahit aetas
in medium ratioque in luminis erigit oras.
Namque alid ex alio clarescere et ordine debet
artibus, ad summum donec venere cacumen.

LUCRETIUS : de Rer. Nat. V. 1448.

INTERNATIONAL
LABOUR   LEGISLATION

BY

H. J. W. HETHERINGTON, M.A.

PROFESSOR OF PHILOSOPHY AT THE UNIVERSITY COLLEGE, CARDIFF

METHUEN & CO. LTD.
36 ESSEX STREET W.C.
LONDON

First Published in 1920

TO

MY FATHER AND MOTHER

WHO

IN PRIVATE AND PUBLIC DUTY

HAVE PROVED THE WAYS OF

NEIGHBOURLINESS AND PEACE

PREFACE

A^T the close of the International Labour Conference, at Washington in November, 1919, Mr. H. B. Butler, the Secretary-General of the Conference, suggested to me that I might write its history. Since, however, an official verbatim record of the proceedings is to be published, it seemed a more profitable expenditure of the time which I could give to this task to attempt not so much a detailed examination of the debates and transactions of the Conference, as a brief exposition of its province, structure, and achievement.

I have therefore written this short account of the International Labour Organisation, of which the Conference is the legislative authority, and of its relation to the purpose and fabric of the central instrument of the new international order, the League of Nations. My main desire has been to stimulate interest in these embodiments of the international idea, and to awaken, in what measure I can, public concern for our responsibility towards them.

The greater part of the book is expository, first of the constitution of the Organisation, and secondly of the circumstances and enactments of the Washington Conference. But I have allowed myself some freedom of analysis, comment, and even of criticism. I have also added some observations on the general problem of international labour legislation. It will be understood, of course, that no officer of the Labour Organisation, and for that matter no one else, has any responsibility for what I have written.

Four appendices are given which may be useful for reference : (1) the text of Part XIII of the Treaty of Versailles, which is the Charter of the Organisation ; (2) the list of the Delegates to the Washington Conference ; (3) the Conventions and Recommendations passed by the Conference; and (4) a list of the members of the Governing Body of the International Labour Office.

It will be agreed, I think, that hopeful as is the initial achievement of the International Labour Organisation, the most significant thing about it is that there exists even now, in this distracted world, a sufficient community of will and of interest to make its establishment possible. Its constitution bears the marks of the divisions that still persist within this common will : and those who framed the Charter of the Organisation did well to take account of them. The growth of a living spirit of unity among men, and of agreement in the ways of promoting human good, cannot be forced. This kingdom is only impaired by violence. But this elaborate system of checks and balances is not itself the ideal. Its creation settles no single problem ; it provides merely the environment within which men's minds and wills may meet and work together, not only in the solution of particular difficulties, but to the creation of a more confident, more generous, and more universal attitude of mind, that shall be free to create and to sustain a more just and flexible and yet more stable international and national social order. The good will must incarnate itself in living institutions ; it can grow only by means of outward embodiment. The supreme function of the Labour Organisation and of the League is just to serve as such a temple of the spirit of mutual care and service, and thereby to give that spirit room, and power, and opportunity for growth. Achievement is the best of all educational disciplines : and the Labour Organisation has important and specific tasks to undertake. But far more important, because far more fundamental, than any particular achievement is the development of that common will and understanding which, if the achievement is won in the right way, it may symbolize and strengthen. One's great hope for the Organisation and the League is that their success will be as much in the inward task of focusing, supporting, and instructing the common will and hope of men for justice and peace as in the sphere of outer enactment. It is a battle of the spirit that has to be won.

I have to thank Mr. Butler and Mr. E. J. Phelan, of the International Labour Office, for reading and criticizing my manuscript, and for much friendly assistance in every way. With characteristic kindness, Sir Henry Jones has spent much more time on the essay than its modest pretensions deserved : his criticism has helped me greatly. I should also wish to take this opportunity of expressing my indebtedness to the

Council and Senate of my College for so readily granting me
the leave of absence which enabled me to accept an invitation
to join the Secretariat of the Washington Conference.

H. J. W. HETHERINGTON

UNIVERSITY COLLEGE, CARDIFF
April, 1920

CONTENTS

INTERNATIONAL LABOUR LEGISLATION

Chapter I

THE GENERAL PROBLEM OF INTERNATIONAL LABOUR LEGISLATION

THE year 1919 saw the inauguration of a system of international legislative, administrative and judicial institutions, to which was committed the task of creating and sustaining a more wisely ordered and stable scheme of international relations than that of the pre-war era. One element of this system, the Inter-*The Congress* national Labour Organisation, achieved the *of Paris.* distinction of entering into active and not unhopeful life before the year had closed. On January 25th the Peace Conference, in session at Paris, appointed a Commission on International Labour Legislation. On April 11th a Plenary Session of the Conference, receiving and approving the report of the Commission, authorized its incorporation as Part XIII of the Treaty of Peace. On October 29th, in pursuance of the terms of the Treaty, the first International Labour Conference assembled in Washington.

That the first international body to come into effective operation was expressly concerned not with political questions of the old order, but with problems of industry and with the conditions under which the ordinary citizens of the world work and live, is significant not more of the shifting of the centre of interest in our modern civilization, than of the new estimate which statesmen are inclined or compelled to place on the views and requirements of the working population. The cynic and idealist can each find in these simple outer facts justification for his reading of human motives and human history : and it is part of the business of this book to furnish the materials on which a judgment may be based. The time has not yet come for any final, or even definite, estimate of the significance of the establishment of the new Organisation. Its future depends on the play of forces far larger than any which it itself can control. But its brief history is, in its own way, an illuminating chapter in the enterprise of constructive internationalism, to which our generation is committed : and incomplete though it is, it is worthy of record.

The problem and the spirit of the Peace Conference have by now been copiously canvassed : and only the broadest and most obvious features need engage us here. Whatever may have been the private inclination and ambition of the chief plenipotentiaries, they were made vividly aware of the full tide of two conflicting movements in the world, with both of which they were bound to reckon. The one was the resurgence of the spirit of nationalism, jealous of every restraint on national sovereignty. The other was the spirit of internationalism, born of the perception that if, in future, the world were to be delivered from the disastrous cataclysm of war, it was imperative to end the tradition that every matter of policy should be left for final determination to the untrammelled jurisdiction of the separate Sovereign States. The two currents of opinion might conceivably have been reconciled, and each have reinforced the other. But that was a task for which the circumstances in Paris were not propitious : and which, in the event, proved to be beyond the resources of the Conference. The adjustment between them assumed the form of compromise and balance ; and it was in this spirit that the Conference framed the new instrument for the regulation of international affairs—the Covenant of the League of Nations.

We have not here to ask whether the authors of the Covenant achieved all that was genuinely open to them, nor, except as concerns our immediate interest in the Labour Organisation, whether or not they rightly discerned the conditions under which the League could discharge the functions committed to it. It is sufficient to record—what, when all is said, still remains an ineffaceable event in the progress of mankind—that in all matters which might affect the peaceful relations of one State with another, every signatory of the Treaty of Peace accepted an obligation to restrict, in some way, its hitherto unlimited right to decide its own policy.

Among the matters which were held thus to be of more than purely national concern, was that of the regulation of working conditions. The reasons for this decision are clear enough. It was not merely an idealist impulse expressing itself in the desire for the achievement of a more humane and generous standard of life over the whole world, and anxious to mobilize to that end all available resources and experience. No doubt that impulse played its part. But besides that, to any sober calculations of the causes of war, it has always been plain that these causes are usually, in part at least, economic. When Napoleon urged his ragged battalions to the conquest of the Lombardy plains, he touched one of the primeval springs of human conflict. Great differences in standards and modes of living are as potent to cause mistrust and enmity between nations as between individuals or classes. Often enough, no doubt, such differences are the outcome of inevitable differences in the natural endowment of countries or of peoples, which are not remediable by any process of external adjustment. On the other hand, even on this fundamental ground, men are not entirely without resource. For, in the face of such natural differences, it is still true that over any large area, within which there exist tolerable freedom of communication and homogeneity of civilization, standards inevitably tend to approximate. They approximate simply because populations tend so to adjust themselves and their relations as to equalize the access of the sources of wealth. The method of making these adjustments has hitherto been partly by migration, and partly by violence—the forcible transfer of some part of the economic resources of one country to its rival. There is little doubt that, if men have the will to apply it, a more excellent method is practicable. It should be possible, first to prescribe certain common minimum standards for all countries, and then to facilitate, by peaceful exchange, a redistribution of material, skill and population, so that at least there is no intolerable privation anywhere in our civilization, and a rough equation is maintained between the resources of any group and the demand which it has to meet. It is a difficult task, soluble only by organised intelligence and good-will. And there is in it scope enough for the full service of an International Labour Organisation.

The genesis of the Labour Organisation.

This, perhaps, is the broadest and most profound aspect

of the work of the Organisation : and it is significant that, very early in the proceedings of its first assembly at Washington, it came in sight of these problems of the adjustment of the flow of workers from one country to another, and of the distribution of raw materials among the industrial nations of the world.[1]

But there are other considerations which indicate how the condition of the working population may affect the world's peace ; and, apart from all questions of the comparative wealth of different countries, implicate all in the internal economy of each. Our modern civilization is extraordinarily sensitive. No considerable unrest can occur in any part of it which does not draw to itself the eyes and hopes and fears of different classes in all other countries. No new sort of social experiment can be undertaken without affecting social relations everywhere. Whatever may be thought of their policy, it was a perfectly sound instinct that led the Allied statesmen to believe that the existence of a Bolshevist Russia would react on the political fabric of every other country. And it is clear enough that, if major transformations take place in any national economy—as, sooner or later, they must where any great part of the population is living below an attainable standard of human well-being—they take place at the risk of international war. Hence the justice of the declaration of the Treaty of Peace, that " conditions of labour exist, involving such injustice, hardship and privation to large numbers of people, as to produce unrest so great that the peace and harmony of the world are imperilled."

Moreover, it is clear that the rate of progress of any one country in the direction of improving working conditions is not independent of the rate of progress in others. Within certain limits, higher standards of living reflect themselves in higher costs of manufacture. It is true that an improvement in the standard of living is often accompanied by a greater productivity, and almost always by a greater skill in the finer forms of manufacture. High wages do not necessarily mean high labour costs. Nevertheless, at our present level of skill in industrial organisation, it does not often happen that full advantage is taken of " the economy of high wages." That would matter comparatively little if each nation were a self-contained economic unit. But, in fact, all nations depend

[1] See pp. 75 et seq.

to some degree on foreign trade : and fluctuations in the volume of foreign trade have a profound effect on the stability and prosperity of national industries. No industry which depends on a foreign market, and no industry which is subject to competition, at home or abroad, from a similar industry in another country can regulate its policy, or determine the conditions under which its operatives work, entirely without reference to the conditions prevailing elsewhere. The quite legitimate fear of inability to meet the competition of foreign industries, working under less favourable, but less costly, conditions, often serves to prevent or to delay the adoption of desirable improvements. Hence, again, the Treaty might fairly hold that " the failure of any nation to adopt humane conditions of labour is an obstacle in the way of other nations which desire to improve conditions in their own countries."

It is true that a certain school of economists, or rather of political theorists who base their doctrines on what they take

Alternatives and prior experiments.
1. Non-interference.

to be the teachings of economic science, are not persuaded that these facts furnish any occasion for concerted national or international regulation. The theory is that by leaving all adjustments to the direction of the natural play of economic interest, each country would find itself engaged in that branch of production for which, by endowment or inheritance, it was best fitted : so that by exporting the surplus of its " natural " manufactures or products, and importing what it lacks, it would contribute to, and share in a maximum productivity of the world as a whole.

It is unnecessary to enter into the philosophical or historical merits of such a theory. Clearly, it has only a somewhat remote relevance to the actual tendency of the world's practice. Every State to some degree insists on controlling its economic life, with a view to certain extra-economic ends—its national self-sufficiency, for example, or the maintenance of a stable numerical balance between urban and rural population, or the encouragement or restriction of industries which are held to be socially advantageous or otherwise. For reasons good or bad, the regulation of industry by national authorities is a permanent feature of our civilization. And the attempts to solve the various problems which have just been indicated, will proceed along lines of regulation, and not of non-interference. The choice before us is not between international regulation and no regulation at all ; but between regulation conducted exclusively by separate national authorities, with an eye solely to their own interest, and regulation designed and carried through co-operatively by all such authorities in consultation with each other, and aiming at the welfare as much of all groups as of any single one.

The instrument which nations have normally employed to control the direction of their economic development has been the Tariff : and the use of the tariff has been 2. *Tariffs.*   (very properly) defended by many of those who were most eager to maintain and to improve the standard of life of industrial workers.   It is plain that, if all other means fail, a tariff on imports (or a bounty on exports) may enable an industry to maintain better standards for its operatives in cases where the competition of the product of less favourably circumstanced workers abroad would either weaken the industry or lower the standard.

The tariff, however, is an instrument which suffers from certain obvious defects.   From the point of view of international peace, there is a permanent menace to friendly relations between States in the existence of an instrument, the use of which may at any moment destroy a great part of a neighbour's trade, and which is always capable of being employed by one State in such a way as to discriminate against another.   It is inevitable, especially in the absence of any kind of competent and authoritative international organisation, that even where in a particular tariff proposal no discrimination or aggression is intended, the suspicion of it is easily provoked.

And, from the point of view of the separate States, and especially from the point of view of the workers in each State, there are disadvantages in the fiscal instrument.   The political consequences of tempting various industrial interests to bargain for concessions to themselves are plain.   But there are purely economic disabilities.   A tariff secures a market to a group of producers, and thereby guarantees that their industry can support a particular standard of life for the operatives.   But it does so by raising prices to a point at which, normally, the great majority of producers in the country, good and indifferent alike, can profitably market their output. The results are twofold.   Prices may easily rise to a level which the worker believes to neutralize the advantage secured to him by this system.   And, inevitably, in the profits of

the more favourably situated employers there is a considerable margin of rent which (except perhaps in the case of a
monopoly) there is no certain way of transferring to the
workers. The workers find, therefore, that a tariff system is
apt to strengthen the position of the employers more power-
fully than their own : and though they may make their
inferences without any very exhaustive analysis, they find
confirmation of their belief in the fact that, on the whole,
the political and economic entrenchments of capital are
stronger in protected than in unprotected countries.

It is natural then that the Trade Union and Labour movements have, as a rule, preferred to approach the problem of
3. *Inter-* safeguarding their national standards from
national another angle. Their instrument has been
Trade Union international Trade Union action. Their belief
action. was that if the Trade Unions concerned with
particular industries could agree on, and enforce,
international minima, then international exchange could be left, in the main, to take care of itself.
At all events the standard of life of the workers in any
industry within a particular country would not be threatened
by the pressure of competition of much less favourably
circumstanced workers elsewhere.

Therein, of course, lies the germ of the idea of safeguarding
industrial conditions by international organisation. It was
comparatively easy to advance from this position to the idea
of an international legislature, composed not only of trade
unionists, but of all the interests concerned, which should
prescribe minimal industrial standards. Evidently, if such a
body could be constituted, and especially if it were given such
a status that its enactments received the authoritative
support of the different Governments, the position would be
much more secure. The decisions of an international trade
union conference, in the nature of the case, can hold only in so
far as the national unions are able to enforce the agreed policy
on their own Governments and employers. The decisions
of an officially constituted international conference would
depend on no such hazardous condition, and might well
come into effective operation without any preliminary
struggle.

Experiments in this direction had been made before the
war. Various unofficial international bodies had attempted
in connexion with particular problems to promote

The begin- uniform or similar legislation in different
nings of countries. Thus, between 1910 and 1914, the
International International Association against Unemploy-
Organisation. ment, with its sixteen national sections in
Europe and America, arranged various conferences to consider Unemployment and kindred subjects.
Mr. Louis Varlez, the Secretary of the Association, is now,
appropriately enough, a member of the staff of the
International Labour Office.   Similarly, since 1889, there
has been in existence an International Permanent Committee
on Social Insurance, a body concerned with the study of the
principles of sickness and accident insurance, and their
application internationally.   The most important of these
bodies, however, was the International Association for
Labour Legislation.

This Association did much useful work in the exploration
of the possibilities of international labour legislation. It
conducted—largely through its separate national sections—
a good deal of research, publishing the results in a periodical
bulletin.   It assisted also at the inauguration of the first
large experiment in the international regulation of working
conditions.   At the instigation of the Association, the Swiss
Government in 1905 invited all Governments to appoint
technical experts to a Conference at Berne, to consider certain
problems connected with the protection of workers against
industrial disease or accident.   As a result of discussions,
draft Conventions were passed prohibiting the use of white
phosphorus in the manufacture of matches, and prohibiting
the employment of women at night.   These Conventions
were remitted officially to the Governments concerned, who,
in the following year, sent representatives to a further
" Diplomatic " Conference. After amendment by the second
Conference, the Conventions were communicated to the
various Powers by the Swiss Government, and were
subsequently ratified by many of these Powers.   The
Convention of white phosphorus became effective in forty-
four countries, that on the employment of women in
twenty-five.

Again in 1913, by a similar procedure, a Conference of
technical experts met to consider problems of the employment of women and young persons.   Draft Conventions,
providing for a ten-hour day for these workers, and regulating
the employment of young persons at night, were passed.

But the outbreak of the war prevented the holding of the diplomatic Conference, which should have put these Conventions into final shape. In stimulating the interest which led to the holding of these meetings the Association did excellent pioneer work, and there is no reason to doubt that if the cause which it existed to promote had not received formal·international recognition in the Peace Treaty, it would have had an increasing measure of success. But the range of its influence was necessarily limited by its " unofficial " character. A Convention is essentially a Treaty : and can, therefore, be drafted only by official representatives of the contracting Governments. Hence the cumbrous procedure which the Association was compelled to adopt. It had to rely on the good offices of one Government to summon the Conferences ; and each enactment had to go through two separate assemblies. There was, moreover, no obligation on any Government to participate, or to pay any attention to Conventions which were adopted. A comparison between the machinery which had to be used by the Association—the only possible machinery for a voluntary organisation—and that provided by the Treaty, shows the very important advance that has been made. Both on the legislative and administrative sides the procedure is much more direct and official in character ; and has behind it much more weighty sanctions. That is a consummation of its efforts which the Association itself warmly desired. And, in recording the progress which has been achieved, it is fitting to record also the debt of those who drafted the Labour section of the Treaty to the work of the Association. Without the experiences of the Berne Conferences, the task of forming the Labour Organisation would have been more difficult. It was, therefore, with justice that, at the close of the Washington Conference, Monsignor Nolens, the representative of the Dutch Government, celebrated the pioneer work of this and its allied organisations.

The act of the Paris Conference, therefore, though it was a new beginning, was yet at the same time the logical culmination of a series of efforts. The problem had long been recognized and various approaches to a solution had been explored. It seemed clear enough that the line of organised international co-operation was at least free from certain difficulties that beset other solutions. The end of the war, and the consequent creation of new instruments of international government, furnished the opportunity to test this solution on a far larger scale than had hitherto been practicable. With the signing of the Treaty, therefore, the principle of internationalism in the regulation of Labour conditions was formally accepted by the great Powers of the world, and accorded external and authoritative embodiment in the establishment of the International Labour Organisation.

We have considered the circumstances which led to the acceptance of the international solution. The *Possible* main circumstance is just the inadequacy of *Criticisms of* other solutions. And it is important to realize *the Inter-* that this line of approach may itself be open *national* to certain objections and difficulties, all the *Solution.* more serious because of the authority with which the new organisation is invested.

The difficulties most commonly urged are those of practicability and procedure : but it is proper to recognize that they may cut more deeply than that. In *1. Uniformity* principle, it may be held it is wrong to try to *not desirable.* impose on all countries the same level of industrial conditions. Differences of national temperament and genius reveal themselves as much in different forms of economic organisation and different habits of industrial life as in anything else : and to enforce uniformity of conditions on countries which differ widely in civilization and ideals, is to risk giving to some civilizations a more definitely materialistic direction than is native to them. Equivalence in working conditions necessarily involves approximation in modes of economic organisation ; and economic organisation reacts upon national character and destiny. The slow-moving, unambitious and peaceful civilization of China, for example, is the expression of a type of mind and genius remote from the restless energy and pugnacity of Europe, and even of Japan. Chinese industrial methods—slow and inefficient as they may seem to Western eyes—are yet integral to their civilization. The leisurely habits, the primitive implements, the looseness of organisation, are all part of the Chinese scheme of life. No doubt there is waste and poverty. No doubt it would be easily possible for China to raise very greatly the standard of comfort ; and that is as desirable there as elsewhere. But surely the worst way to remedy these defects is to approach the Chinese situation, not from the Chinese point of view, but from a consideration of its reactions upon other and divergent types of life.

Assume, e.g., that a limitation of hours is imposed upon the Chinese cotton industry—not primarily in the interests of the Chinese operatives themselves, but in order to safeguard the standards won by Lancashire or French, or, for that matter, Japanese workers.[1] The effect would be, of course, that in order to maintain their industrial position, the Chinese employers—often enough not native Chinese at all—would try by every means of " speeding up " to secure within the shorter working day the same product as under the older system. And with every limitation imposed on China, another step would be taken in the direction of assimilating not only Chinese conditions, but necessarily the structure and habits of Chinese industry, to Western models. The enforced industrialization of China would be the inevitable end—an end, the effects of which in China itself and on the rest of the world no one may lightly assume to be good. The defect of all international action is that since, *ex hypothesi*, it considers every problem from the standpoint of international, rather than national, effects, it may easily make for a breach in the continuity of national practice and tradition. At the best, it must often happen that a nation, especially a nation assumed to be industrially " backward," has to make changes in its economic organisation for which it is not entirely prepared, even materially ; at the worst, it *may* happen that a nation is compelled or encouraged to adopt a type of economic organisation that is really alien to its temper, tradition and ideals.

This, of course, is an extreme but by no means an impossible example. And it is perhaps not a sufficient answer to reply that, as the text of its Constitution stands at present, the International Labour Conference has no power to enforce on any country a change which that country's Government does not desire. If, as may be hoped on other grounds, the Conference succeeds in acquiring prestige and authority enough to make any Government reluctant to traverse any of its decisions, it will be even more difficult for such Govern-

[1] At the Washington Conference, the Japanese employers' representative pointed out the necessity of securing in China some reduction in the hours of cotton operatives corresponding to the reductions made in Japan. But he did not press for any immediate decision on the point, and supported the decision that the Chinese Government should be asked to study the situation with this end in view. (See p. 69.)

ments as are here chiefly in question to resist its recommendations.

There is, it may be admitted, a real danger here. Diversity in personal equipment and character among its members is an asset of the first importance to any community—national and international alike ; and respect for the " personalities " of different states is a fundamental condition of wise international ordering.

The danger is one against which it is difficult to provide any formally effective safeguard. Article 19 of the Charter of the Organisation prescribes that "in framing any recommendation or draft convention of general application, the Conference shall have due regard to those countries in which climatic conditions, the imperfect development of industrial organisation, or other special circumstances, make the industrial conditions substantially different ; and shall suggest the modifications, if any, which it considers may be required to meet the case of such countries." This provision, though it does not cover the whole ground, expressly recognizes the principle of differentiation, and gives play to the discretion of the Conference. And, in truth, the only real safeguard against the tendency to produce artificial resemblances in industrial practice is just the good sense of the Conference. It would be wrong to hold that the interest of an International assembly in conditions within any particular country is confined to the international effects of those conditions. The Treaty clearly enjoins upon the Conference the consideration of problems, not only from the point of view of international peace, but from that of a disinterested desire for the betterment of working conditions everywhere.[1] And though it is always easy for men to consider first how interests specially committed to them are likely to be affected by any proposed change, it is an unduly cynical view of the history of legislatures to suppose them incapable of any lively or genuine disinterestedness. The success of the Conference's efforts to legislate internationally depends entirely on its avoidance of two dangers—sectional nationalism and doctrinaire equalitarianism. If there should ever predominate a tendency on the part of national groups to consider any suggestion *solely* from the point of view of their own interests, or, on the other hand, if the abstract principle of equality of conditions governs the decisions of any large

[1] See Preamble, pp. 113-4.

section of the Conference, then it is probable enough that such legislation as the Conference contrives to impose on " backward " states will wear an artificial aspect ; and may well be harmful in results. If both these considerations—entirely proper and relevant both to the constitution and business of the Conference—are held in due subordination to the sympathetic study of the economic, historical and moral conditions of each country for which the Conference legislates, there is no reason why, in the spirit of this part of the Peace Treaty, the necessary and appropriate adjustments between State and State should in any grave way menace the preservation of the characteristic civilizations of the different peoples.

It is difficult to say whether there is added security or danger on this point in that, roughly, and with all necessary qualifications, it may be said that each of the sins into which the Conference is liable to fall is a special temptation to a different group represented in it. The employers are reasonably apt to regard things primarily from a national standpoint. To them, in our present economic order, has been entrusted the organisation of production and distribution ; and in this respect they carry a special responsibility to their own countries. They are naturally first preoccupied to see that no condition is introduced which would make their work impossible, and imperil the continuance of the service which they have undertaken to render. On the other hand, the dogma of equalitarianism is in its own way specially attractive to the workers. A reformist movement, especially one which is designed to protest against unnecessary differentiations of wealth and opportunity, tends naturally enough to crystallize its creed into a formula ; and the formula of " equality " has long exercised a peculiar fascination over the politically minded. It was easy to see the operation of both these tendencies in more than one debate at the Washington Conference. The most apposite for our present purpose, perhaps, was that on the regulation of hours of work in Japan. The matter must be referred to later. But the essence of the situation was just that a very strong demand was made by the Labour group[1] for the application to Japan

[1] The one dissentient from this view among the Labour delegates was Mr. G. H. Stuart-Bunning, of Great Britain. It was naturally difficult and ungrateful for Mr. Stuart-Bunning to dissociate himself from his colleagues on an important issue like this. But there can

of the same limitation of hours of work as were to be pre-scribed for Western countries. This demand was supported by the Italian employers' representative, on the ground that Italy had introduced an eight-hour working day, and it was therefore only reasonable that Japan should do the same. The two motives, in this instance, were quite clear : the desire on the part of the workers to enforce not merely a substantial reduction of hours in Japan, but at once, and without over-much regard to existing conditions, to achieve their ideal as fully there as elsewhere—and on the other hand, the desire of the employer in the interests of his employees as well as of himself to secure that his own operations should have no greater restriction placed on them than those of his fellow employers in other countries.

Sometimes, as in this instance, the play of these two tendencies may help to impel both groups in the same direc-tion ; but normally, perhaps, each group will tend to act as a check upon the other. In any case, it is clear enough that either tendency, however desirable and proper in itself if it became a dominant motive in the deliberations of either group, might easily produce results that were open to criticism along the lines that have been indicated. It is, perhaps, fortunate from this point of view that the delegates of the Governments are in a position to exercise a preponderating influence on the decisions of the Conference ; and it is plain that in this matter, as in the others, they have a special duty towards the Conference and the ideal which it embodies. In the end, as has been said, there is no adequate safeguard against this danger except the conscientiousness of the Con-ference itself in legislating not in an abstract, cosmopolitan fashion, but in the full sense of the term internationally, in such a way as to support and reinforce every element of value in the native culture and character of its constituent members. It must do its work deliberately ; and after a full study of the conditions and aims of every State-member of it, realizing well that economic conditions alone do not shape the destiny of peoples ; that nations, like individuals, cannot live by bread alone. Whether it can do this, only the future can declare. The signs at Washington were

hardly be any doubt that his action was both wise and helpful, and that it was a useful example to his colleagues, not indeed to limit their ideals by existing facts, but at least to study the degree of their immediate applicability. (See p. 71.)

not wholly reassuring ; though neither were they wholly ominous.

There is, perhaps, one further consideration that should be borne in mind. Apart altogether from the possible effects of an international legislature, other and powerful forces are definitely making for the industrialization of the East. Japan, for good or ill, has set herself to become a nation of the same material power in the world as the nations of the West ; and has already gone far enough on that way to make it certain, both that she will not abandon that enterprise, and that other Oriental countries will develop, though less rapidly, in the same direction. Japan's action, especially during the war, has accelerated the pace of industrial development in the East ; but it is probable enough that that development was bound to occur sooner or later. It is hard for the more enterprising members of any nation to forego the prospect of considerable material gains which the introduction of large-scale industrial production offers to them, and the increasing commerce of East and West gives them every opportunity to understand the possibilities. And the obvious economic advantage of many vigorous and powerful interests in the West itself lies in the industrialization of the Orient. Their activity can be regulated, but can hardly be prevented. Under the stimulus of their own ambitions and the pressure of those external forces which operate in this direction, Eastern countries will almost inevitably develop within themselves a productive organization not essentially dissimilar to that of the West. And if that is so, it is surely well that their apprenticeship in industry should be less hazardous than that which most European countries have undergone. It is a great gain that, at the beginning of this phase of their evolution, they should be associated in some official assembly with those who can witness to the hardly won lessons of Europe, and show what safeguards have been proved by experience essential to the health and welfare of industrial workers. Every nation and every generation has to buy its own saving experience ; for men are extraordinarily loath to learn from others or from the past. But at least it may be possible to secure that the price is not disastrously high, and that the worst mistakes of the West are avoided.

In the second place, it may be argued that even if this difficulty of principle be set aside, the practical

2. *Inter-*   difficulties in the way of international legislation
national   on labour conditions are insuperable.   There
regulation   is   no   uniformity   in   the   situation   and
impracticable. resources of different countries.   They vary,
                 not only in ideals, temperament and habits
of life, but in climate, in the possession of raw materials,
in technical skill, in degree of economic development, and
in organizing power.   It is impossible to devise any uniform
law, except one so general as to be almost insignificant, that
could apply even to all Western countries alike.   And if
it be sought to work out equivalent rather than uniform
legislation, would that not be better done by the different
Governments themselves, with such assistance or even
stimulus as may be derived from international conferences
of the old, unofficial kind, between the interests concerned ?
Is it not the case that even in political entities of a federal
type it has been found necessary to assign the power of
legislating on labour conditions to the state or regional
rather than to the federal or central authority ?   It would
seem still more impossible to commit the duty of such legislation to an international body.

Now while it is important to realize the difficulties which
such a new departure in legislative institutions must face,
and while it is well that all concerned in it should understand the limits of what it may hope to achieve, it may be
suspected that this argument proves too much.   It amounts,
in effect, to a simple *non possumus*.   And that is precisely
the type of argument which has been brought against any
general labour legislation even within the area of a single
country.   In every discussion of the problem of a minimum
wage someone has shown the impossibility of prescribing
a minimal standard, or series of such standards, to all the
diverse types of industry in one country.   But no one now
seriously believes that any such impossibility exists.   The
early debates on the British Trade Boards are full of fore-
bodings as to the results of the attempt to achieve even in a
single industry within one country something approaching
an equality of conditions.[1]   Yet Trade Boards are a firmly
established and expanding part of our industrial apparatus ;
and no great difficulty has appeared in their working.   A
universal regulation of hours of work was long regarded as
impossible ; but the present Government—hardly to be

[1] See " Hansard," 1909 : 24 March ; 28 April ; 16 July.

described as adventurous—is committed to an almost universal eight-hours bill.

The complexity of all these questions is greatly increased when they are dealt with on an international scale ; and it seems fairly certain that for many years to come some of them—as, e.g., that of wages—cannot advantageously be the subject of any general legislation. But there may still remain a large range of problems on which international discussion, agreement and legislation are perfectly practicable. The same fundamental problems of industrial organisation tend to appear in all civilized States, and the same methods of solution have to be explored. Most States have a great deal of common experience ; they find the same kind of difficulties or definite evils arising out of similar conditions. There is, perhaps, less disagreement among nations than among interests within one nation as to the main features of a desirable industrial organisation. Especially, perhaps, on what may be called the secondary or ameliorative work of labour legislation, there will certainly be found room for a good deal of common action, in matters like insurance, safety-devices, the exchange of workers between different countries, and the treatment of the special problems which occur in the normal development of many or all industrial workers—adolescence, motherhood, sickness or accident, old age. None of these matters perhaps touches the basic problems of industry ; but, in sum, they determine a great deal of human happiness or misery. When the Conference has tested its powers in relation to these concerns, it may be able to proceed with some assurance and some hope of success to other more critical and penetrating issues.

There is, indeed, no certain *à priori* method by which the possible achievement of an international legislature can be defined. Its limits, like those of any national government, can be settled only experimentally. In some important ways the limits will necessarily be more circumscribed than those of a national State. On the other hand in some important, though, perhaps, not equally fundamental ways, they will be wider, just because, as we have seen some reason for thinking, there are some significant problems that will yield more readily to international than to national treatment.

There are other possible criticisms of the method of international approach, plain enough even on a summary review of the position, but of which it is difficult to

3. *Further*   assess the force without the test of practice.
Objections.   Employers in general may resent having restrictions imposed upon them at the instigation of an assembly so ignorant of their special needs and opportunities. But it is hardly likely that such resentment could survive an exact appreciation of the *(a) From the* position. Employers, as such, are represented in *employers'* the Conference itself, and before any enactment *side.* of the Conference can become a national law, employers have a further opportunity to expound the difficulties with which they will be faced. Moreover, employers in any one country are likely to feel less objection to accepting a restriction which is intended similarly to affect their fellows in other countries. A more serious point may emerge from the side *(b) From the* of the workers in advanced or rapidly advancing *workers' side.* industrial countries. The aim of such an international assembly will be to prescribe international minimal standards. And these standards are likely to be nearer those prevailing in the worst-situated countries than those of the best. The pace of a team is more nearly that of its slowest than of its fastest member. The effect will be that the international standards will always be less satisfactory than those which have been secured by the independent action of the workers of the more progressive countries ; and the rate of advance in international legislation will be slower than that which they might hope to secure through their own national organisations. Employers, therefore (and Governments), will always be equipped with an additional and forcible argument wherewith to resist demands for improvement in conditions. They will be able to point to the fact that the standards already prevailing in an industry are above the prescribed international standards, and perhaps above those established in other competing countries.

Some part of the objection, at least, rests upon assumptions which may or may not be fulfilled. It is true that the pace of a team is little above that of its slowest member, but only where the team has to move as a single body. And there is nothing either in the spirit or in the enactment of the International Labour Organisation which requires uniformity of conditions or of progress. It is indeed expressly enjoined that the standards prescribed are minimum standards and are to be construed neither as implying any reduction of higher standards already achieved, nor as prohibiting any country to prescribe standards as much in advance of the minimum as it thinks fit.[1] Moreover, it is not certain that the enactments of the Conference will, in every case, conform more nearly to those of the least advanced country than to those of the best. Washington furnished more than one striking instance to the contrary.[2] And although, in general, the assumption implied in this criticism may be true as regards such basic conditions as those of hours and wages, it need not be true of the considerable range of what has been called secondary enactment. So far as the Washington experience goes, it showed a tendency on the part of the Conference *not* to base its standards on the lowest actually existing, but rather to prescribe as high a standard as seemed to be possible, and to admit a system of delays, so that the less advanced could reach the desirable condition not by one leap but by a series of timed and graduated steps.

Nevertheless, when all is said, there is still some force in the contention ; and it remains for the future to declare how seriously the workers will feel the objection. It is reasonable to expect that it will not be found substantial : and, in all likelihood, the organised labour movement in the more advanced countries will be willing to risk the result of whatever handicap may be imposed upon them for the sake of their international ideals.

Experience may well reveal further difficulties ; and, indeed, until the Organisation has been put to a more protracted test, it is impossible to know how *Conclusion.* serious are those which have been here considered. But it is something that the test will be made. There is a critical problem set for solution by the Organisation ; and, so far as our analysis carries us, it is one which can be solved in no other way. The founders of the Organisation approached it, mainly, though not exclusively, with a special preoccupation in mind, the relation of that problem to the maintenance of international peace. The Organisation has been planned from this point of view ; and it must be judged first as participating in the system and purpose of the League. But there is, in a sense, a larger measure, and the final verdict on its achievement will weigh not only the part which it plays in this high enterprise of

[1] Cf., last clause of Article 19.   [2] See pp. 86, 89, et seq., 93.

sustaining a better international order, but its promotion of positive human good in the sphere in which it has direct competence.

There is recorded in the Treaty of Peace a series of declarations of principle on the status and conditions of labour to which all the signatory States have pledged themselves.[1] They constitute a kind of charter of the rights of the workers in every country. It is something of a commentary on our civilization that it should have been thought worth while to record formally a system of principles which no humane person would regard either as disputable or complete. But it is still a fact that nowhere in the world are these principles effectively operative, and no country yet thinks of bringing its industrial system first to the test of how far it secures to all who participate in it the rights herein prescribed. The formal acceptance of these principles is itself not without significance. They can be translated into practice only by the action of the separate States and of the interests within each State. But the process may be greatly assisted by the existence of an international body specially charged with the guardianship of these principles, with the co-ordination of the experience of all nations in their application, and with helping to bring to birth a national and international order governed by them. That, in brief, is the function of the International Labour Organisation.

[1] See p. 128.

CHAPTER II

THE STRUCTURE OF THE INTERNATIONAL LABOUR ORGANISATION—THE CONFERENCE

THE Organisation thus created consists of two parts: a General Conference of Representatives of the Members—an assembly charged with functions which are legislative in character; and an International Labour Office, whose duties may roughly be described as executive. The whole machinery, as we have *General* seen, is planned as part of the League of Nations. *Structure.* The details of its relation to the League will emerge in the course of discussion. It is sufficient here to note that all members of the League must accept the prescriptions of the Labour part of the Treaty and enter upon membership of the International Labour Organisation : and on the other hand, it is clear that all members of the Organisation must also be members of the League.

It will be convenient to treat in this chapter, and those immediately succeeding, of the International Labour Conference. The Office and its functions will concern us later.

The Conference is composed of representatives of each of the States which are members of the Organisation. The representatives of each State—four in number— *The Inter-* fall into two equal groups—governmental *national* and non-governmental. Two delegates are *Labour* appointed by each Government as representing *Conference.* itself, the remaining two delegates, though appointed by the Government, represent the organised employers, on the one hand, and the organised workpeople on the other. The Members undertake to nominate non-government delegates " chosen in agreement with the industrial organisations, if such organisations exist, which are most representative of employers or workpeople, as the case may be, in their respective countries." These four delegates from each State are the members of the

3   21

Conference proper and they alone have the power to speak and to vote. But each delegate may be accompanied by advisers, chosen in the same fashion as the delegates and " not exceeding two in number for each item on the Agenda of the Conference."[1] These advisers may, under certain conditions, replace the delegates at the Conference and exercise the full rights of membership. They may also act for the delegates on Commissions and Committees set up by the Conference. Each delegate to the Conference votes in his own individual right. Every country, therefore, which is fully represented at the Conference casts not one, but four votes ; and each of the votes is cast, not according to the view of the majority of the country's representatives, but by each delegate separately, voting for himself and expressing his own judgment. The deliberations of the Conference are directed to the drawing up of Draft Conventions or Recommendations. For the adoption of either, a two-thirds majority of the delegates present is necessary, and on any matter a valid vote requires the participation of at least half the delegates attending the Conference.

Each of these points requires some little commentary. We may consider them in order.

The first point concerns the composition of the delegations from each State. There is written plainly in this provision the lesson of the war-time experience of all countries. It would have been hard, prior to 1914, to secure the assent of most of the Governments of the world to the inclusion in an official international legislature of representatives of non-governmental interests. But the places assigned to the delegates of the employers and the workers in the Labour Organisation correspond exactly to the part which these interests took in advising upon, and even in sharing responsibility for, the industrial and labour policy of many Governments during the war. The process was carried further in Great Britain and in the United States than in other countries ; but to some degree it operated in all. It is, perhaps, noteworthy, though it need cause no surprise, that in the international organisation the right of these interests, and especially the right of

Commentary.
(1) *As to the composition of delegations.*

[1] A further provision relating to advisers is that " when questions specially affecting women are to be considered by the Conference, one at least of the advisers should be a woman."

the workers to have some share in legislating upon labour
conditions, is more explicitly recognized than it is still within
the boundaries of some of the State-members.   Nevertheless,
the first criticism that is often passed upon the constitution
of the organisation is that it has not gone far enough in this
direction.

At the Peace Conference, the French, American and Italian
members of the Commission on International Labour Legislation pressed for the equal representation of all three
constituent elements of the Conference.   They believed it
to be unlikely that the Conference would command sufficient
moral authority among employers and workers, and especially

(*a*) *On
Government
predomi-
nance.*

among the latter, if any predominance were
accorded to the Governments.   Plainly the
composition of the Conference makes it possible
for a combination of the Government delegates
and those of another group to carry enactments
which are bitterly resisted by the third group.
No doubt what was feared was an agreement between the
Government and employers' groups on a much more conservative policy than that which commended itself to the
workers ; so that not only would such a policy receive whatever sanction attached to the findings of the Conference,
but the Conference itself would suffer serious discredit in
the eyes of the workers.   The point was long in dispute, and
in the end the arrangement which was embodied in the
Treaty was carried by a bare majority.

The case for the majority's decision, however, is sufficiently clear.   A further clause in the constitution of the
Conference, to which attention will be drawn later, prescribes
that, in the end, the decision as to whether or not the enactments of the Conference shall become the law of any participating State, rests with the Government of that State.   Under
these circumstances, it is clear that it would be useless for the
Conference to pass enactments which did not command the
support of the Government delegates.   A Government
may refuse to accept a Convention for which its representatives had voted ; but it is almost certain to refuse one passed
against their will.   It was therefore probably a wise decision
which gave to the Government representatives acting as a
whole an absolute veto on any proposal, and which threw
upon them a special measure of responsibility for the policy
of the Conference.

The Constitution as it stands does this. Not only are the Government delegates in a position to mediate between the possibly widely divergent views of the other groups, but they are in a position to ensure the practical acceptance of any proposal which is so framed as to attract a substantial measure of support from either or both of the other interests. Under the present arrangement neither of the non-government groups is able to impose an absolute veto on any proposal ; neither party therefore can effectively pursue the policy of insisting on a choice between its maximum demands and nothing at all. It is always worth while for both to concede sufficient to attract Government support ; so that there is a continuous incentive to try to reach a practicable working arrangement.

And that conclusion is not overturned by the fact that the Government delegates are bound, in the nature of the case, to be a much less homogeneous group than the delegates of either the employers or the workers. The sympathies of each Government delegation may incline, according to the political complexion of the Government, more to one side than to the other. But in every case they represent, not a party, but a Government which is, to some extent, implicated in their votes, and to which they may be called upon to justify their action. At Washington nothing was more obvious than the responsibility which the Government delegates as a whole felt, or the part which they played in shaping the policy of the Conference. The Conference was unmistakably in earnest. The hope of practical results depended on its reaching decisions which could be supported both in the Conference itself and before their home Governments by the Government delegates. The result was a prolonged and serious endeavour, largely under the influence of Government representatives, to arrive at decisions which could command a considerable measure of support in all parties.

It would take us too far afield to enquire whether the same result could have been achieved by another form of constitution. The main fact is that that result was achieved by the present form of constitution, and that, so far at least, it survived the critical test of practice. It would be interesting to discover which of the two interests, employers or workers, gained by the preponderance of the Government representation. In the discussions at Paris the workers were somewhat reconciled to the adopted constitution by the reflexion that

Labour was steadily acquiring greater political power in all countries, and might soon hope, in many, to assume the responsibility of Government. But even at present, so far as the Washington Conference is any guide, it seems that the constitution of the Conference is, on the whole, more favourable to the workers than to the employers. If one compares, say, the proposals of the employers and of the workers on the problem of the limitation of hours of work, with the Convention on this subject which was finally adopted by the Conference, one finds that the Convention corresponds more nearly to the desires of the workers than to the desires of the employers ; and the same is true of other Conventions. The explanation, of course, does not lie wholly in the composition of the Conference, but it is symptomatic of the fact that the Government delegates, as a whole, were not disposed to load the scales in any way against the workers.[1]

It is possible, however, that a more serious objection may be raised to the composition of the Conference than any which seems to have been discussed in *(b) On the* Paris. It may be held that a Conference *tripartite* constituted by Governments, employers, and *division.* workpeople, represents a very transitional form of industrial organisation. Governments themselves, for example, are large employers, and will probably become even larger. On the other hand, if the universal impulse towards the " democratization " of industry comes to any measure of fulfilment, the status of the employer— whether Government or private—and the status of the worker will undergo a radical transformation. The workers, collectively, will undertake some of the most important duties of the employer ; the employer will become, not a separate " interest " in industry, but the repository of a clearly defined function. The Government, whatever its ultimate responsibility for industry, will have little to do with the detailed

---

[1] It is difficult to support by specific facts this impression, that on the whole the preponderance of Government delegates operated favourably to the workers. The only votes which can now be analysed are the " record " votes—the votes which were taken by roll call. As these were taken mostly on the question of the final adoption of a Convention or recommendation, and were often almost unanimous, they are not specially instructive from this point of view. But a comparison of results actually reached with the programmes of the different interests, gives considerable support to the view here expressed.

regulation of the conditions under which industry is carried
on, and no special competence in the matter. If such a
transformation does ultimately take effect, then an assembly
such as the Conference, which is based on the present
differentiation of interests among the three constituent
elements, will cease to embody any clearly recognizable or
relevant principle.

The exact weight to be given to this contention depends
on one's view of the rate at which these changes in industrial
organisation are likely to eventuate. It is hardly a serious
criticism of any institution that its present basis will not
always be satisfactory, unless, indeed, that basis has been
prescribed unalterably for all time. Such, however, is not
the case in this instance. Changes of structure may be
difficult, but they are expressly provided for,[1] and the Conference can at any time take the initiative in this direction with
a reasonable assurance that any change which it strongly
desires will be effected. Under those conditions, the only
question which arises is as to whether or not the constitution
of the Conference will sufficiently sustain it during the period
of growth to that level of maturity at which it can safely
undertake the work of self-criticism and modification. On
that issue there can be no serious doubt. The Conference
may not survive ; but if it fails, it will not be because of any
inherent constitutional weakness, but because the tide of
public affairs sets too strongly against any genuine internationalism. Great changes may well take place in the
structure of industry during the next decade. But it seems,
on any reasonable view of the probabilities, that the tripartite
division will not seriously misrepresent any possible industrial
organisation. The " workers " will still be those who find
their main, but not their sole, preoccupation in the day to day
business of production ; the " employers "—no doubt a
greatly broadened class—will represent the organising,
technical and administrative staffs, with an experience and
point of view characteristic of their functions, and different
from that of the operatives. The " Government "—as appears even from the little we can learn of the Soviet system—
must represent an interest different from either of these—
at the least, the interest of consumers rather than of producers,
and (on any intelligible theory of social organisation) the
integration of the economic interest of society with the

[1] See Article 36.

complex of other interests and institutions which are the soul and body of a civilized community. It is likely enough that, for as many years as we need reckon on, the basis of representation will be found satisfactory enough. Such change as may be necessary will be in the proportionate weight to be assigned to each interest rather than in the definition of the interests themselves.

The second point of importance is the form which the Treaty prescribes for the election of delegates to the Conference, and the right of individual voting at the Conference itself which it confers on all members. These provisions were clearly designed to secure to each constituent interest indisputable freedom to express its point of view. All delegates —and advisers—must be appointed by the Governments and accredited by them to the Conference. But a Government cannot appoint a non-Government delegate against the express wishes of the most representative organisation of the interest which he is assumed to represent. A Government may—if it can—attempt to influence the choice of these representative organisations ; the Treaty does not confer upon them the right of independent election. It gives only the right of veto : in that no one can be accredited to the Conference as their representative without an expression of their consent. In effect, of course, this does secure in a country in which organisations of workers and employers are strong, the right of nomination. The non-Government delegates and advisers of Great Britain, for example, were nominated by the National Federation of Employers' Organisations on the one hand, and by the Trade Union Congress on the other. It is, no doubt, possible that either of these bodies might on some occasion nominate a delegate to whom the Government felt serious objection. If both parties persisted in their attitude, so that no appointment approved by both sides could be reached, no legitimate nomination could be made. The Treaty makes it certain that in such a contingency a Government has the right to refuse to make any election at all ; the result of which is to disfranchise at the Conference, not only the party to the disagreement, but also the other non-Government interest.[1]

2. Methods of appointment and freedom of voting.

[1] Under Article 4 : " If one of the members fails to nominate one of the non-Government Delegates whom it is entitled to nominate, the other non-Government delegates shall be allowed to sit and speak at the Conference, but not to vote."

It is clear that some points at once difficult and important may arise in the carrying out of these electoral provisions ; and the matter is significant enough to merit consideration. The Washington Conference gave some illuminating experience on the point, and it will serve both the purposes of record and of our immediate discussion if we review the possibilities in the light of the Conference transactions.

It is evident from the brief discussion above that the Treaty contemplates the failure of a Government to nominate a representative of one or other of the remaining constituent interests. But it does so only in the case in which the Government and the organisation most representative of the interest concerned, cannot arrive at agreement in the selection of a delegate. It does not permit a Government to refuse to make an appointment on any other ground than that of its unwillingness to accredit the person selected. In principle, there is an equal obligation on the Government to elect non-Government as to elect Government delegates. Such clearly is the intention of the Treaty : though it does not appear that there is any effective means of compelling a Government to live up to its obligations. If, for quite insufficient reasons, a Government persistently refused to accredit the nominee of one or other of the non-Governmental organisations, it would of course inflict a permanent disability on the other organisation ; but it would retain its right officially to take part in the Conference by means of its own representatives. The danger, perhaps, is so slight as hardly to be worth providing against.

(a) On the failure to appoint non-Government delegates.

But this difficulty can occur only in cases in which there is, within the country concerned, genuinely representative organisations of employers and workpeople. In cases where no such organisation exists, the position is necessarily different. Under these conditions, failure to appoint non-Government delegates cannot be held to imply any obvious remissness on the part of a Government in the fulfilment of its obligations.

As it happened, there were at the Washington Conference several delegations consisting only of Government representatives : and the Conference, at the instigation of the Labour group,[1] gave some attention to the problems raised by their

---

[1] The motive of the Labour group, of course, was concern at the even greater preponderance which such a condition gave to the Government representatives.

presence. The Commission which examined the question of Conference procedure[1] inquired of each such delegation the reason for the absence of non-Government delegates.   In most cases the explanation lay in certain temporary difficulties—insufficient time to take the necessary steps, or the failure of a duly appointed delegate to make the journey to Washington.   But in one or two cases there was found to be some misapprehension of the obligations of Governments on the point.   And in a third group of cases, the Governments pointed to the non-existence within their areas of the representative organisations specified by the Treaty, and asked for guidance as to their procedure.   This case is clearly the most difficult.   The Commission took the view, subsequently endorsed by the whole Conference, that while in cases where the appropriate industrial organisations existed, participating Governments were under an unequivocal obligation to appoint representatives of these as well as of themselves, in cases where these did not exist, Governments should not be pressed to appoint the full number of delegates.   If they were, it is clear that the practical result would be to give these Governments four delegates instead of two : for the two ostensibly unofficial delegates would be, in fact, nominees of the Government.

The decision was clearly wise ; but what was most instructive in it was the insistence with which all sections of the Conference were disposed to require that wherever an election of a *bona fide* representative of an industrial interest was possible, such an election was obligatory on participating Governments.

" The credentials of Delegates and their advisers shall be subject to scrutiny by the Conference, which may, by two-thirds of the votes cast by the Delegates present, *(b) On competing claims* refuse to admit any Delegate or adviser whom *to nominate* it deems not to have been nominated in accordance with this Article."[2]   By this clause, *non-Govern-* the Conference is enjoined to satisfy itself that *ment* the Governments have observed the appropriate *delegates.* procedure in the appointment of delegates : and in a matter which touches so definitely the authority of the Conference, it is desirable that the scrutiny should not be merely formal. Manifestly no question can arise concerning a properly accredited Government delegate.

[1] The Commission on Standing Orders.   [2] Article 3, clause 7.

But in relation to non-Government delegates, two different questions may emerge. What the Treaty requires is, as we have noted, that the nomination of the employers' and workpeoples' representatives shall be made in agreement with the most representative organisation of these interests where such organisations exist. In this matter also, therefore, two types of cases occur : the first relating to countries where representative organisations exist, the second to countries where they do not.

The Washington Conference rightly thought it worth while to secure a more than perfunctory scrutiny of delegates' credentials, thereby establishing a most healthy and important precedent. One of its first acts was to appoint a Commission on Credentials, consisting of a representative of each of the three sections in the Conference.[1] Cases of both types were considered by the Commission ; and its report on these cases was the subject of a lengthy debate in the Conference.

In the first category came the protests which were made in respect of the elections of the workers' delegates of France, South Africa and the Argentine Republic ; and of the employers' delegate of Cuba. In all these cases, organisations sufficiently broad to be considered representative were admitted to exist : but it was alleged either that the Government had not consulted any organisation at all, but had made the nomination on its own account ; or that it had made the nomination in agreement with an organisation which was in fact less representative than another competing organisation. Obviously the questions raised were questions of fact ; and might be supposed to be capable of easy determination. Had the Governments in question consulted an organisation ? If so, was that organisation the most representative which it could have consulted : and in particular was it more representative than that on behalf of which the protest was made ? The question resolved itself simply into one of arithmetic : and in three out of the four cases, was so settled to everyone's satisfaction. But, curiously enough, the only protest which was carried to a division in the Conference—that on the Argentine workers' delegate—belonged to this apparently simple class.

The second category plainly raises more difficult issues.

[1] The representatives were Sir Malcolm Delevingne (Great Britain), chairman ; M. Carlier (Belgium), and M. Oudegeest (Holland).

The Government of a country in which no such representative organisation exists may reasonably refrain from appointing any non-Government delegates : but if, nevertheless, it does appoint delegates purporting to express the views of employers and workers, the Conference must have some assurance that, conformably to the spirit of the Treaty, the delegates are authentic representatives of the non-Government constituencies. It was the election of the Japanese workers' delegate which brought the Conference face to face with this issue. The circumstances were these.

There are some four million workers in Japan, 30,000 of whom belong to the Japanese Federation of Labour. The Government took the view that an organisation *—the case* which comprised less than 1 per cent. of Japanese *of Japan* workers could not be considered " representative " in any serious sense of the word. It therefore devised a special method of election. The workers in every town were invited to assemble in order to elect delegates to a provincial meeting : the provincial meeting in turn appointed delegates to a meeting of the whole Empire : and this meeting selected three names, one of whom was appointed by the Government as the Labour delegate. A protest was lodged by the Japanese Federation of Labour against this procedure on the grounds (*a*) that the Government had brought undue influence to bear on these series of meetings, so that the delegate finally appointed was not a *bonâ fide* workers' representative : and (*b*) that, in any case, the Federation itself, though small, was what the Treaty required —the most representative organisation in the country, and ought therefore to have had the right of nomination.

Evidently it is a defect of such a method that, under it, it is easy for a Government to exercise improper influence ; and though such a charge is necessarily hard to prove, it is important that every opportunity should be accorded to the complaining party to make it good. In this instance no detailed evidence was laid before the Commission : and every member—including the Labour representative—was satisfied that the charge could not be sustained. There remained, then, the second ground—the contention that, in the circumstances, the whole procedure devised by the Japanese Government was irrelevant and therefore invalid. On this issue the members of the Commission held divergent views. The Government and employers' delegates were of

opinion that the action was justified : the Labour representative, while agreeing that the Japanese Government
had seriously tried to conform to the spirit of the Treaty,
and accepting the view of the majority that on this occasion
the Japanese Labour delegate should not be excluded from
membership of the Conference, still held that the duty of the
Government was to have recognized the right of the Federation
to nominate the delegate. In this opinion he was supported
by a resolution of all his Labour colleagues, who entered in
the Record of the Conference an expression of their view that
in future the Japanese Government should appoint the
Labour representative in agreement with the Japanese
Federation of Labour.

This insistence may appear somewhat pedantic. But
it is instructive because there is a principle of real importance
behind it. One of the declarations inscribed in the Treaty
is that freedom of organisation should be enjoyed for all
lawful purposes, by employers and workpeople alike. And
this declaration is construed by the workers as signifying
the successful ending of the long Trade-Union struggle for
" recognition." They believe, also, that the acceptance of
that principle commits the Governments, if not to the positive
encouragement of Trade Unions, at least to a policy of passive
benevolence. They suspect, however, that some Governments are still disposed to make no more than a verbal
confession of faith : and that under such Governments the
weakness of Trade Union organisation is due, in part at least,
to the hostility of the Governments. They desire, therefore,
to make it a positive injunction to all Governments that they
shall confer on the existing Trade Unions whatever prestige
they can ; and shall translate formal " recognition " into
an effective right to play a part in national and international
labour affairs. The establishment of a special electoral
procedure for the purposes of the Conference operates directly
against this policy. However reasonable it may be in itself,
therefore, the workers prefer that it should not be employed
in any case where an authentic workers' organisation, however
small, is in being.

There is, of course, a great deal of substance in this contention, and it seems worth while to state it fully, because at
Washington there appeared to be a good deal of misapprehension as to the real ground of the workers' objection. And
the reason why the objection to the Argentine delegate was

carried to a division was just that that protest, though in appearance one of simple fact, in principle raised the same issue.

The delegate to whom objection was taken was unquestionably a *bona fide* representative of the workers.   He had been nominated by the Argentine Railway Workers' Union—an old-established union of 15,000 members, covering all parts of the country. There exists, however, in the Argentine Republic a General Federation of Trade Unions, which, though it covers a greater variety of occupations than the Railway Union, draws its membership exclusively from a few large industrial provinces.   The size of the Federation was in some dispute ; the protest claiming 80,000 members, the Government admitting 20,000. The Federation was clearly in all respects, except in geographical distribution, the more representative body of the two ; and, failing agreement between the rival organisations, it ought to have had priority.   The Conference may have been wise, after a debate, to accept the majority recommendation of the Commission that no action should be taken on the present protest, but that the Argentine Government should be recommended for future Conferences to endeavour to effect some arrangement with both Unions.   Some laxity may be justifiable on the occasion of the first Conference. But the Conference will pretty certainly be wrong if on subsequent occasions it fails to reject a delegate nominated in a fashion similar to that disclosed in this instance.

It is probable enough that the Labour group would have been content with this declaration and would not have sought to bring the issue to a vote, had it not been for the further circumstance that of the two competing Unions, the Railway Union was legally incorporated, the Federation, though not illegal, was not incorporated.   The implication was that the Government favoured the smaller Union because it was more conservative in policy and more easily amenable to official influence, while it passed over the larger Union because of its assertion of independence.[1]   An action which cannot

—the case of the Argentine Republic.

[1] The speech of the delegate of the Argentine Government in the debate contained a charming instance of the effect of natural environment on characteristic metaphor.   He remarked that the General Federation of Labour existed only to celebrate the Russian Revolution, and to call periodic general strikes, " which in Buenos Aires excite no more attention than an earthquake."

clear itself from a suspicion of this kind strikes directly at the principle on which the Conference is founded : and though the Labour motion to reject the credentials was defeated,[1] it was, no doubt, a sound tactic formally to draw attention to the situation. The majority vote was indeed indefensible, except on the ground that with a novel organisation like the Conference a certain degree of misunderstanding of constitutional niceties was pardonable.

These instances have been set down in some detail because the issue is, in its own way, fundamental. The Conference will inevitably be prejudiced if there should be any disposition on the part of Governments, either through ignorance or indifference, to evade the obligations which the Treaty imposes upon them. The untrammelled right of the most representative organisation to participate in the election of its delegate, and the absolute freedom of a duly accredited delegate to speak and vote independently, are at the root of the constitution. For some time to come it is to be expected that these matters will give rise to difficulty ; and in many cases it will be hard to decide whether or not a Government has done all in its power exactly to carry out its duty. At the moment, the difficulties are more likely to affect the workers' side than the employers' ; but the position may shortly be reversed. And, in either case, it may easily happen that at the very outset of a Conference the prospect of any useful work will be imperilled by a sharp division of opinion on rights of membership. The only safeguard is a rigid determination on the part of all sections of the Conference to see that the obligations are both understood and fulfilled. It is, no doubt, an ungrateful and embarrassing task for the representatives of one Government to challenge an official action on the part of another Government ; and the Conference would suffer if the defendant Government withdrew entirely from participation. But it would suffer much more seriously, and in the end disastrously, if it failed securely to establish the tradition of independent representation which is clearly the purport of the articles of its foundation.

The third point of our summary requires only the briefest note of explanation. The legislation which the Conference enacts has to be embodied either in Conventions or in Recommendations. The legal status of these two forms

[1] By forty-four to twenty-six. The minority contained a proportion of Government votes.

3. *Form of*   is somewhat different ; but, up to a point,
the acts of   they impose the same obligation on the par-
the Confer- ticipating Governments, and require from the
ence.   Conference the support of a two-thirds majority.

The difference between them is partly one
of sanctions,[1] and partly one of detail. A Convention is
understood to be drafted in such a shape that, without
substantial alteration, it can be accepted by the different
States as part of their national law. A Recommendation,
on the other hand, is simply a declaration of principle or of
policy, in greater or less detail, which States are asked to
adopt and to translate into the legislation appropriate to the
special circumstances obtaining in them.

The occasion which gave rise to this differentiation in form
was the constitutional disability of certain federal States in
Labour legislation. In the case of the United States, for
example, it was contended at Paris—though there was a good
deal of dispute on the point—that the federal Government had
no direct competence in this matter, since power to legislate
on labour conditions is reserved almost entirely to the State
Governments. The Government of the United States therefore would not undertake to ratify Conventions drafted by
the Conference, on the ground that it had no power to commit
the State Legislatures. The way out of this impasse was to
devise a form of procedure which would leave open to the
United States Government, or to any Government in the
same position, some other course than the choice between
entire acceptance and entire rejection, which are the
alternatives normally contemplated in the case of a
Convention. The Recommendation is this form. The duty
of a Government in relation to a Recommendation is to
consider whether it will or will not pass legislation embodying
the principle enunciated therein. In cases, therefore, in which
the power of a federal authority to enter into Conventions
on Labour matters is subject to limitation, the Treaty leaves
it to the discretion of the federal Government to treat
Conventions to which such limitations apply, as Recommendations only.[2] Thus, in the instance under consideration, the

[1] See below p. 38 et seq.
[2] Article 19, clause 9 : It is to be observed that this right extends
only to cases in which the federal authority has no legal competence.
If a Convention is passed on any subject which is within this jurisdiction of the federal Government, then that government must regard
the Convention as a Convention, and not as a Recommendation.

Government of the United States would not ratify, say, a Convention on Hours of Work, but would undertake to forward it as a Recommendation to the State Legislatures, and invite them to take action in accordance with its terms.

When the instrument of the Recommendation had been devised to meet this exceptional case, it was realized that its use need not necessarily be thus restricted. There may well be many subjects on which the Conference is ready to accept a definite policy, but on which detailed legislation by the Conference would be either extremely difficult or inexpedient. In such cases a declaration of principle in the form of a Recommendation may be a convenient and valuable form of procedure. It seems highly probable that on many subjects the first step towards the initiation of a Convention will be the drafting of a Recommendation. That course would assist the process of crystallizing opinion and practice, which is a necessary preliminary to detailed legislation.

CHAPTER III

THE STATUS AND SANCTIONS OF THE ENACTMENTS OF THE CONFERENCE

THE most crucial question for any international organisation is as to the status of its enactments and the sanctions which can be attached to them. At the preliminary discussions in Paris two different views prevailed. The Belgian, French and Italian members of the Labour Commission desired that the Conference should be invested with the same mandatory powers as are enjoyed by any national legislature. They proposed that Conventions duly enacted should be binding upon all participating States, whether or not their representatives at the Conference had assented to the Conventions. A State which dissented from any finding of the Conference should have the right to appeal against that finding to the Council of the League of Nations ; and the Council might refer the Convention again to the Conference. But if the Conference reaffirmed its previous decision, no further appeal should be allowed.

1. Proposal that the Conference should have mandatory powers.

This, or something like it, perhaps, embodies the ideal at which an international legislature ought to aim. But, since it had been decided that at least on some important issues such a status could not be conferred on the League of Nations itself,[1] it was clearly impossible to accord it to the Labour Organisation. The Labour Commission, therefore, in sympathy with the views expressed by the delegations mentioned, recorded a resolution expressive of its hope that, as soon as was possible, an agreement would be made endowing the Conference " with power to take, under conditions to be determined, resolutions possessing the force of international law." But, at the moment, it was constrained to frame a procedure investing the Conference with less exalted powers.

[1] See Article 12 of the Covenant of the League.

4

or if the reply is thought to be unsatisfactory, the Governing Body, after publishing the complaint and the reply, may request the Secretary-General of the League of Nations to appoint a Commission of Enquiry.[1] This Commission is to be chosen from a standing panel of experts, and is to contain three members, one representing each of the constituent interests of the Conference. None of these three may belong to a State directly concerned in the complaint.

The Commission of Enquiry is bound to make full investigation of the complaint ; and all the Members of the Organisation, whether parties to the dispute or not, are pledged to assist it with all the information in their possession. It has to render a decision on all matters of fact, and make Recommendations as to the steps which should be taken to remove the cause of complaint. It is also charged to indicate in its report the economic measures which might appropriately be instituted against the Government in question, if it should refuse to carry out the recommendations of the Commission. The Secretary-General of the League has then to communicate the report of the Commission to the Government concerned, which must indicate within a month's time whether it accepts the recommendations contained therein. If it declines to acquiesce, it may elect to refer the whole dispute to the Permanent Court of International Justice ; or, if it does not so elect, any other Member may do so.

This Court has power to hear the whole case de novo ; and to deal with the findings of the Commission of Enquiry as it may see fit. But its report is final. The report must contain recommendations as to the action necessary to meet the complaint, and as to the economic measures appropriate in case of default. If, in the end, the Government concerned still refuses to carry out the recommendations of the Commission, or of the Court, any other Member of the Organisation is free to take against it the measures indicated in the report. These measures may remain in force until the defaulting Government informs the Governing Body of the Office that it has taken the necessary remedial action, and its statement

[1] There appears to be, in the charter of the Organisation, a curious (and inexplicable) difference between complaints received from industrial organisations and complaints otherwise initiated. In the first case, the duty of the Office is confined to publishing the complaint and the (unsatisfactory) reply. But, plainly, the matter could not rest here. It would necessarily be raised in one of the alternative forms which would compel the Office to carry it further.

has been confirmed by a procedure similar to that adopted
to pronounce on the justice of the complaint.

It is easy to see that this elaborate procedure covers a
position of real weakness. In the end, the International
Labour Organisation has no power of compul-
4. *Comments.* sion. The final sanction which supports the
obligations devolving upon its Members lies
not within its own control, but in the control of the Members
acting on their own initiative. There is no undertaking
that the Members will jointly apply to any recalcitrant
Government the economic measures indicated in the Reports.
And, plainly, if matters ever come to this point, there is
no great likelihood that any effective action will be taken.

The economic weapon in general has serious defects.
Some time must necessarily elapse before its pressure is
felt by the State against which it is employed ; and it may
easily happen that its use will be more costly to the State
which employs it than to that against which it is employed.
If, under these circumstances, there is no clear understanding
that the weapon will be used jointly by all States, it is in the
highest degree improbable that any one State will be ready
on its own account to inaugurate the use of it. In this
respect the Labour Organisation seems to be less adequately
equipped than the League.[1] Before its authority can be
regarded as satisfactorily established, it will be necessary
to secure an undertaking from the Members that they will
jointly put into operation the appropriate economic measures.
This degree of authority is still substantially less than that
contemplated by those who advocated the investment of the
Conference with the full status of an international legislature.
For it leaves intact the freedom of each Member in the first
instance to accept or reject the enactments of the Conference.
But it would at least provide a firm sanction for the obligations which any Member had deliberately accepted, and
relieve every Member of the unpleasant choice between
failing to support the Organisation when a clear breach of
obligation was declared to exist, and initiating on its own
account, and against another Member, measures of whose

[1] See Article 16 of the Covenant of the League, by which
the signatories agree immediately to take steps against a defaulting
member. In other respects the Organisation is more fortunate than
the League. Thus, on a matter of this kind, the action of the Governing Body is not restricted, as is that of the Council of the League,
by the necessity for arriving at a *unanimous* decision.

Chapter IV

THE WASHINGTON CONFERENCE

THE closing sections of the Labour part of the Peace Treaty prescribed the holding of the first Annual Conference at Washington in October, 1919, and laid down the agenda to be considered at that meeting. The duty of convening the Conference was assigned to the Government of the United States of America; and an International Organising Committee was established to assist that Government in making the preparations for the Conference.

The Organising Committee.

The major part of the preliminary work necessarily fell upon this Organising Committee. It was composed of representatives of seven different States, under the chairmanship of M. Arthur Fontaine, of the French Ministry of Labour. Mr. H. B. Butler, C.B., of the British Ministry of Labour, was appointed Secretary. The Committee began its deliberations within two days of the passing of the Labour part of the Treaty, and during the ensuing three months it held frequent sessions in London and in Paris. Its work, though capable of the most summary notice, was arduous : and a great part of the success of the Conference must be attributed to the thoroughness of the preparations made by the Organising Committee in the brief time at its disposal.

It drew up, in the first instance, a provisional scheme of Standing Orders, in accordance with which the whole proceedings of the Washington Conference were conducted. It circulated to all the Governments which were entitled to participate in the Conference [1] questionnaires on the subjects to be considered at Washington, inviting information both as to the existing law and practice on each of these matters,

[1] The forty-five States named in the Annex to the Covenant of the League as original members. Of course, in the case of those thirteen States which were not signatories of the Treaty, the right of Membership of the Labour Organisation was contingent upon adherence to the Covenant of the League : but owing to the early date of the Conference, many States took part in it before their Governments had had an opportunity thus formally to adhere.

and as to the attitude of the Governments towards proposals for reform. On the basis of the data thus available, and of its own independent researches, the Committee prepared a series of Reports, both in French and in English, containing the relevant information, and drafts of Conventions designed to serve as a basis for the discussion of the Conference. These Reports were circulated to all members of the Conference some weeks before its opening, so that the various interests in all participating countries might have an opportunity of reviewing the proposals, and of instructing their delegates as to the attitude to be adopted at the Conference itself.

It may be useful to give here a brief account of the machinery of the Conference. In future, of course, the responsibility for the general administration of the Conference will rest upon the International Labour Office. But in this instance, since the Office had not then been constituted, it devolved upon the Government of the United States. That Government did, in fact, make the arrangements for the housing of the Conference, and for all its mechanical necessities. Congress granted an appropriation of $63,000 towards the expenses: the remainder being found by the League of Nations on the account of the Labour Organisation.[1]

The Machinery of the Conference.

The purely secretarial side, though, of course, until the Conference opened it remained under the general responsibility of the U.S. Government, was, in fact, provided for by the transfer to Washington of the greater part of the staff of the Organising Committee. That staff was reinforced first from Europe by a corps of interpreters who belonged to the League of Nations secretariat, and by a few temporary members, and later in Washington, by representatives drawn from several of the delegations present at the Conference, and many members of administrative departments of the United States Government. Mr. Butler, first as Secretary of the Organising Committee, and later, by fore-ordination and election, Secretary-General of the Conference, was the head, and (it is just to add) the inspiration of the whole organisation.

The staff thus constituted undertook the interpreting and reporting of the Conference, the translation, preparation and circulation of the necessary documents, and the secretarial duties in connexion with the various Committees and

[1] See p. 97.

Commissions which were set up. It was no small burden of work : and in the novel circumstances in which the Conference met, constant demands were made upon the staff by the expected, but unpredictable, emergencies and vicissitudes of its progress. But there was goodwill and energy enough in the international staff to meet every situation : and throughout the whole duration of the Conference no serious difficulty or delay occurred on the secretarial side.

The official languages of the Conference were English and French. A delegate might address the Conference in any language he chose, but the responsibility for the translation of his speech into one of the official languages rested on his delegation. The interpreters undertook the translation from one official language into the other : so that every speech was rendered in at least two languages. The delay imposed on the proceedings of the Conference by the necessity of translating every speech was often wearisome, especially to those who understood both French and English; but after the initial difficulties with the acoustics of the Conference Hall were overcome, the interpreting went with admirable smoothness.

Each day a verbatim record of the proceedings of the Conference was printed in English, French, and Spanish. The Spanish issue was provided specially by the United States Government for the benefit of the delegates of the South American Republics, and proved to be of great service. Later in the Conference an effort was made to have Spanish recognized as one of the official languages. The case for this proposal was undoubtedly strong, since, when all the South American States are taken account of, Spanish is the native tongue of a much larger proportion of the Conference than is any other language. On the other hand, the delay to the proceedings of the Conference which would result from a triple rendering of every speech would have been almost intolerable. The Spanish representatives therefore accepted a compromise solution, to which the Conference readily assented, that while Spanish should not be an official language, it should enjoy at future Conferences the same facilities as were given at Washington.

Difficulties. Time, place, and agenda had all been laid down by the Treaty : and all of them, in their own way, made some little difficulty for the Conference.

The Agenda was long, too long for one meeting of the Con-

ference, and much too long for the first meeting, which had
to give a good deal of its attention to points of
(1) *Agenda.* organisation and procedure. The Conference
accomplished all that was asked of it. But
during the last fortnight of its duration it worked at greater
pressure than is desirable ; and some of its decisions were
taken hastily, without the mature consideration which might,
with advantage, have been bestowed upon them.

The combination of time and place served to enhance this
sense of strain. Washington is many days' journey from
Europe : the end of October is perilously near
(2) *Time.* Christmas, when all good Europeans wish to
be at home. By mid-November it was clear
that the Conference would be reluctant to continue in session
for long after the end of the month. It rose, in fact, on
November 29th. And if, from this point of view, the Conference came too late, on the other hand, and in more important
ways, it came too soon. The space of six months between
April and October gave little enough time for the Organising
Committee to carry out its preliminary researches and to
communicate its Reports to those States which are remote
from Europe. Some delegations, therefore, had had insufficient opportunity to consult the interests which they
represented on the draft proposals contained in the Reports.[1]

Again, the summoning of the Conference in October gave
rise to a curious legal difficulty. The Treaty, under the
provisions of which the Conference met, had not at that
date been ratified ; nor had the League of Nations, of which
the Conference is an organ, entered formally into life. Strictly
speaking, therefore, the Conference had no legal status at
all. It could acquire such status only after the Treaty and
the League came into effective operation. The Conference
extricated itself from the legal difficulty by a device which,
though entirely proper, wears the familiar aspect of a legal
fiction. On November 29th the Conference did not close.
It adjourned, after giving power to the newly constituted
Governing Body of the Office to summon it again, or to take
such other action as was necessary to validate its proceedings.
It was not until January 27th, 1920, that, by the declaration
of the Governing Body at its meeting in Paris, the Conference formally ended. The Treaty had been ratified and
the League of Nations established on January 10th.

[1] They had had, of course, ample time to consult on the general
questions considered.

No doubt, if the Peace Conference had foreseen the attitude of the United States Senate to the Treaty, they would have chosen almost any other place rather than

(3) *Place.* Washington as the stage for the entry of the League into the drama of History. Washington was selected as the meeting-place of the Conference presumably from a desire that this first international legislative assembly should have the prestige and support of President Wilson's presence. Unhappily, just before the meeting of the Conference, the President was stricken with his grievous illness, and America was plunged into the conflict on the ratification of the Treaty. While the Conference sat at Washington, the fight in the Senate reached its climax in the decision to refuse ratification. The Labour part of the Treaty was especially the object of bitter criticism, often less informed than might have been expected in an assembly charged with such grave responsibilities. Competent observers were of opinion that one of the most powerful factors in the whole struggle was the resentment of American manufacturers at the suggestion—a grossly mistaken one, as we have seen— that American industry was to be hampered by restrictions imposed upon it at the bidding of outside nations.[1] One Senator, indeed, protested strongly against the holding of the Conference in Washington at all, and suggested the wholesale deportation of these alien agitators who had come to corrupt the pure citizenship of American Labour.

Under those conditions it was inevitable that Washington should be a sadly unpropitious environment for the inauguration of the new international order. The Conference did its best in the circumstances. Its first resolution invited the American employers and workers to send representatives to take part informally in its proceedings. But except for a fleeting appearance by Mr. Gompers, no representative came, and no public interest, except a little of the hostile sort, was shown in its work. The Conference, moreover, was inclined to feel at the outset that without American participation the future of the League, and with it the future of the Labour Organisation, were in jeopardy, and its own deliberations possibly of little practical account. The

[1] It is proper to add that at this time American public opinion was much exercised by the long-continued steel strike, and by the national coal strike, and inclined to lay the blame of its troubles on the alleged influence of Bolshevist agitators. This frame of mind, of course, is not peculiar to America.

Canadian employers' delegate, for example, took occasion more than once to express his view that it would be quite impossible for Canadian industry to accept obligations which were not accepted by the United States. It was only later, when experience had given the Conference some confidence in its power and stability, that it was able to recognize as an earnest of its destiny, the declaration which the expression of this opinion drew from the President of the Canadian Privy Council that the Government of Canada, having set its hand to the Treaty, and having accepted the Labour Covenant, was not prepared to make the fulfilment of its undertakings to the Conference contingent on the action of the United States.

In these respects, therefore, Washington was an unlucky choice. But when the whole tale is told there is much to be set on the other side. Climate and natural surroundings were extraordinarily attractive. The Labour Department of the Administration, in the face of public indifference, was sympathetic and helpful ; and in the person of its Secretary, the Hon. W. B. Wilson, it provided the Conference with a Chairman who fulfilled in the most admirable way the duties of that exacting and difficult office. And, most of all, the psychological effect on the Conference of the American attitude to the Treaty was, in the end, greatly to the advantage of its work. When the Conference had acquired sufficient assurance in its own future to realize that it did not wholly depend on American participation, it came to feel, at the same time, a special responsibility for the success of the Washington assembly. It was, for the moment, the trustee of the League in a country which seemed to have little faith in its ideals. It was constrained to show by its own actions that internationalism had become an effective force in the world, and that if the League lost much by the withdrawal of the United States, the United States lost even more. It is quite certain that this crusading spirit helped to hold the Conference together. More than once, when it seemed that divergencies of opinion had become so acute as to make any happy solution impossible, a night's reflection and contact with American scepticism furnished a powerful impulse to the adjustment of differences and agreement on a common policy. Paris would not have elected for Washington if it had known the circumstances. In the event, it could hardly have made a more favourable decision.

at the end of the Washington Conference. By a later decision of the Supreme Council, however, the question of their admission, and of the date of it, was referred to the Conference itself. The Conference thus approached the question with the major issue predetermined. The late enemy Powers had signed the Treaties under a promise of their admission not later than the end : and no member of the Conference showed the slightest disposition to go back on that decision. The only question was as to the date. One voice only was raised in the Conference in favour of adhering to the date originally proposed—that of M. Guérin, of Lille, the delegate of the French employers. The Conference heard M. Guérin with the respect which is due to one who speaks of a great suffering, but it did not waver in its resolution. M. Fontaine, on behalf of the French Government, and M. Jouhaux, on behalf of the French workers, spoke of the necessity of inaugurating at once the new enterprise of full international co-operation, and of the impossibility of excluding two great industrial nations. They won the full accord of almost every delegation at the Conference. When finally the resolution was put to admit Germany and Austria at once to full membership of the Organisation with the same rights and obligations as other members, some few delegates abstained from voting, one voted against, seventy-one voted in favour.

The resolution was at once communicated to the German and Austrian Governments. Both Governments expressed their satisfaction at the decision of the Conference, and undertook full co-operation in its work. The German delegates actually started on their journey ; but they were delayed in Europe by difficulties of transport, and when it became evident that they could not hope to reach Washington in time to take part in the proceedings, the journey was abandoned. The first participation of the late enemy Powers in the International Labour Organisation was therefore post-poned until the meeting of the Governing Body of the Office in Paris at the end of January, when the German members were present.

It was, perhaps, a happy issue for the Conference. It had made the fitting gesture when it admitted the Central Powers without delay to membership of the Organisation. But their welcome could not have been cordial : and it was hardly a misfortune that, through no fault either of the Conference or of Germany, that country was represented only by the space at the Conference table which had been reserved for its delegation.

The one disadvantage which the Conference suffered from this decision was its repercussion on the debate on the remaining applications. Several such applica-
(2) *Other* tions had been received, or were put forward
Applications in the Conference on behalf of States which were not included among the original members of the Organisation. Most of these applications were, however, unofficial, in the sense that they were not made directly by the Governments concerned, with an undertaking to accept the obligations of membership. These, therefore, called for no serious consideration. But the Government of Finland had made formal application to the Supreme Council ; and the Council had remitted this application, together with those of Germany and Austria, for the decision of the Conference.

No difference of opinion existed as to the desirability of admitting Finland to membership : and, obviously, since the requests of Germany and Austria, which came before the Conference in the same form as that of Finland, had been favourably considered, it was at first sight impossible to justify a refusal in the case of the smaller and friendly State. Nevertheless, the Commission which considered the application was unable to arrive at a unanimous decision, and presented two reports to the Conference—a majority report supporting the admission, a minority report opposing it. The minority view was, in a word, that, desirable as it was that Finland should be admitted, the Conference had no power to grant the request. Membership of the Organisation was defined and provided for in the articles of its Constitution. The only qualification for membership recognized by the Treaty was membership of the League : no other mode of entry was prescribed or even contemplated. Finland, therefore, could acquire membership only after admission to the League ; and though the Conference would be fully justified in admitting Finland to informal participation in its work, and in expediting by all possible means the admission of Finland to the League, it could not constitutionally admit to membership of itself. The fact that the Supreme Council had forwarded Finland's application, might imply that in the judgment of the Council the Conference had power to admit. But since the Council was not the body charged with the interpretation of the Treaty, its opinion could not justify the Conference in taking a decision which was clearly beyond its competence.

The report in which Mr. Rowell, of Canada, developed this constitutional argument, and the speech in which he defended it, were certainly among the most masterly of all the statements laid before the Conference. On the constitutional question, there could be no two opinions that he had all the better of the argument. The one practical defect in his case was that it amounted to a pretty clear demonstration that the Conference, in admitting Germany and Austria, had acted in excess of its powers. It is true that the Treaties with these Powers were signed on the understanding that they would be admitted to the Organisation independently of their admission to the League, and that before the signature of the Treaties the Supreme Council, which gave this undertaking, was itself competent to render an interpretation. On the other hand, the Supreme Council had no serious right to enter into an engagement which was clearly incompatible with the terms in which the Treaty was drafted ; and when the Conference had chosen to be guided by the Council's interpretation in the one case, it was difficult to refuse its leading in the other.

There was the further difficulty that, as the League of Nations had not then been established, no authoritative interpretation of the Treaty could be given,[1] nor could the procedure for the admission of Finland to the League be initiated without vexatious delay. In the light of these considerations the Conference was evidently strongly inclined to support the majority argument. But, as it happened, thanks to the ingenuity of a Belgian delegate, an intermediate solution was found agreeable to both parties. The Conference accepted, in principle, Mr. Rowell's view of its constitutional powers ; and agreed that, after the formation of the League, admission to membership should be effected only through admission to the League. But, until then, without thereby creating a precedent, and subject always to a revision of its action after an appeal to the Court of International Justice, the Conference might properly act on its own responsibility, and admit Finland not merely to informal participation in the Conference, but to full membership of its present

[1] The power to interpret the Labour Covenant lies with the Court of International Justice. (Article 37.)

session, on the same terms as those other countries which had not formally adhered to the League.[1] This decision, of course, did not give Finland all that it had asked. It carried with it no right to membership of the Organisation, and no right to participate in future Conferences, except after a similar process of special admission or after admission to the League. But it secured that Finland suffered no disability at Washington. Its representatives were full members of the Conference : and presumably before another Conference comes round, Finland will have been admitted formally to the League, and will, therefore, ex-officio, belong to the Organisation. At a later date an official application was received from the Government of Luxemburg, which the Conference accepted in the same form as in the case of Finland.

The debate on this issue was of a high degree of intrinsic interest. But there are perhaps two points of special significance which call for some little comment. The *Comments.* first is the somewhat disconcerting willingness of the Conference to take a decision which had been amply proved to be unconstitutional. There is no doubt that if the two original reports had been put to the Conference, the view of the majority would have *Attitude of* won overwhelming acceptance. The circum-*the Confer-* stances, it must be allowed, were peculiar. *ence.* The admission of Germany, if the minority case were sound, and in spite of Mr. Rowell's defence of it, was clearly a stretching of the strict letter of the law ; and made it hard to refuse a similar concession to Finland. Nevertheless, the cases were different. Apart altogether from the promise made to the Central Powers *before* the signing of the Treaty, there was no apparent likelihood of their participating in the Washington proceedings. Whatever the legal rights and wrongs of their admission, the whole matter was fairly certain to be set in proper form before the next Conference by their admission to the League. The Finnish representatives were, however, actually in attendance at Washington awaiting admission. They were in a position effectively to participate in the proceedings at once, if they were admitted without any reservation ; and it might easily happen that a Convention or other act of the Conference requiring a statutory majority, should secure that majority by the aid of the Finnish votes. In that event, any

[1] See Footnote, p. 44.

member of the minority had an obvious instrument wherewith to invalidate the decision of the Conference. An appeal against the right of Finland to vote would almost certainly have been sustained. The point was made perfectly clear to the Conference. Sir Malcolm Delevingne, for example, expressly intimated that since a decision to admit Finland would so profoundly contravene the constitution of the Conference, the British Government delegates would be constrained to carry an appeal to the Court of International Justice. But the Conference was apparently quite unimpressed by the risk, and almost light-heartedly prepared to gratify its very laudable sentiment of fairness at the cost of imperilling its constitutional security. It was easy to sympathize with the cause—especially with the strong desire of the Scandinavian States that Finland should at once be admitted to full membership; but it would have been a seriously prejudicial decision. It was somewhat disquieting to find the Conference—all sections of it, but particularly the Labour group—so impatient of the inevitable constitutional limitations of its actions, and so ready to pass over the judgment of its legal advisers. It showed little of the judicial and objective attitude of mind that is necessary to the success of its enterprise. But it is fair to add, first, that there was some weight of legal opinion on the other side; and, second, that the debate arose early in the course of the Conference, before the different groups had had time to understand each other, and when there was still some confusion of purpose.

The second point of importance is the substantial question that was raised as to the nature of the relationship which exists between the Organisation and the League.

(2) Relation of Labour Organisation to the League. There evidently was a strong desire on the part of several delegates to construe the constitution in such a way as to throw into relief the independence of the two institutions. Some, at least, of those who desired to admit Finland supported this course on the ground that the Conference would thereby take advantage of the opportunity offered to it by the Supreme Council to interpret its constitution as that of an entirely autonomous body.

There is, of course, a certain propriety in the view which underlies this contention. The functions of the Labour Organisation and the functions of the League differ broadly, as economic and political. There would, no doubt, be a certain advantage in the clear distinction of the two institutions. Even if, for example, the League failed to become an effective reality, and were destined to dissolution, it is conceivable that the Labour Organisation might survive and continue to do valuable work in the sphere appropriate to it. Or, less probably, though still possibly, the converse might be true. Or again, it is easy to imagine circumstances in which a particular State may be eligible for or desirous of membership of one Organisation, but not of the other. Those cases could not be provided for under the existing Covenants.

On the other hand, the arguments against separation appear to be almost decisive. The distinction between " political " and " economic " functions is not one which can be drawn in any absolute way. Many of the problems with which the Labour Organisation is specifically charged—such, e.g., as " the regulation of labour supply," including presumably the exchange of workers between countries—raise political issues of some complexity ; and political considerations would clearly be involved in any scheme for giving the Organisation powers of coercion against a defaulting member. In the same way, the League's activities must necessarily have direct economic implications. And, finally, the prospect that one Organisation may succeed and the other fail, is somewhat remote. They may well succeed and fail in different degrees. But effective internationalism in any sphere of human activity is bound up, for many decades at least, with the success of the League. If that fail in its primary function of eliminating or restricting international war, there is no likelihood of any prolonged or significant organised international co-operation on behalf of any other interest. It is true that antagonisms are, in the main, less likely to be raised in the progressive regulation of labour conditions than in other problems with which the League must deal. To that extent the Labour Organisation has the prospect of a less hazardous future. But it is well that whatever measure of success and prestige it achieves, should be brought to the support of the League. It is possible, even probable, that the first substantial successes of internationalism will be won in the sphere of Labour legislation ; but the greatest result that could follow from them, and the only guarantee of their own permanence, would be the reinforcement of the authority of the League in the greater difficulties which it must face.

As the Treaty stands, the Labour Organisation, while an integral part of the League, and subordinate to it in point of qualification for membership, yet enjoys, in its own sphere, almost complete autonomy. Except, as has been noted, with regard to sanctions, its organisation is self-contained and self-sufficient. No other part, and no officer of the League, may interfere with the Labour Organisation in the discharge of the specific functions assigned to it.[1] Even in matter of finance, although the League provides for the expenses of the Labour Organisation out of the general funds of the League, and though the League has the right to audit the accounts of the Organisation,[2] it cannot directly determine the amount of the annual budget of the Organisation, or prescribe the forms of its expenditure.

Whether, therefore, by accident or by design, it has so fallen out that the Labour Organisation is largely independent of the League. A comparatively slight amendment of the Treaty would make it completely independent. That, no doubt, is, or may sometime prove to be, a fortunate circumstance. But it is quite certain that, in the present conditions of the world, neither organisation would gain by the separation. Both will require a full measure of mutual reinforcement and support, and that can be best assured when in principle and in fact they are members one of another.

[1] At the moment of writing (March, 1920) it is announced that both the League of Nations and the Labour Organisation propose to establish sections dealing with health. Presumably the Labour section will be specially concerned with industrial hygiene and occupational diseases ; and the two sections will co-operate. But it does not appear that even if the Labour Organisation proposed to set up a health section which the League thought to be superfluous, the League has any power to over-ride the decision.

[2] Article 13, Clause 3.

Chapter VI

THE CONVENTION ON HOURS OF WORK

IT is possible now to give some account of the deliberative
and legislative work of the Washington Conference.
The most difficult and controversial subject with
which it had to deal was the regulation of hours of work.
But, apart from interest of the subject, the debates were
notable from another point of view. This
Procedure was the sole occasion on which the Conference
attempted—unsuccessfully, as it proved—to
legislate in full session. All other matters on its agenda were
referred in the first instance to a Commission for examination
and report. These Commissions, meeting in private, and
having before them the information and suggestions of the
Organising Committee, were able, in most cases, to accomplish
their work expeditiously, and to present to the Conference
a more or less unanimous report. That report was considered,
clause by clause, in full Conference, amended as a rule only
on points of detail, accepted as a whole by the vote of the
Conference, and sent to a drafting Committee of legal experts
to be given the appropriate legal form. In this shape,
either as a Draft Convention, or as a Recommendation, it
was brought back to the Conference for final acceptance or
rejection. At this final reading no debate took place. The
Conference voted by roll call on the Convention as a whole ;
and, as it happened, in every case recorded a favourable
decision by much more than the prescribed statutory majority.
This procedure, on the whole, answered admirably. The
Commissions were so chosen as to contain representatives of
all the sections of the Conference. Any report, therefore,
which was agreed to by a Commission was likely to be built
on lines with which the full Conference would have no fundamental quarrel. In the debate on the Report, any point
of detail could be amended by the Conference ; or any matter
on which the Commission had itself been seriously divided
could be reviewed. On all such matters a two-thirds majority
was not necessary : so that the Convention, as a whole, was

not imperilled by a division of opinion on any particular point within it. Anyone who felt very strongly the unwisdom of a particular decision, could, of course, vote against the Convention as a whole on the final reading, where a two-thirds majority was required. Most of the final votes revealed the presence of a dissentient minority of this kind. But the greater number of the delegates, though disagreeing with certain detailed provisions of a Convention, yet preferred the Convention as it stood to nothing at all : and the requisite majority was never in doubt.

In the consideration of the regulation of hours of work, however, the Conference seems at first to have contemplated dispensing with the reference of the subject to a Commission. Mr. G. N. Barnes' motion, at all events, with which the debate opened, proposed only the establishment of a Commission to consider the application of the Convention to the special cases contemplated by Article 19,[1] in which, by reason of climate or other circumstances, some modification would be required. He proposed also that the Conference itself should take as the basis of its discussion the reports and suggested draft Convention drawn up by the Organising Committee : the implication being that the main Convention, apart from the special modifications, should be made by the Conference.

The motives which led to the adoption of this plan appear to have been twofold. It seemed worth while, in the first instance, to ascertain by experiment how far the Conference was able to legislate as a whole. From this point of view the experiment was a failure, though it would be hard to regard it as a crucial test. The debate became extraordinarily confused : and so many complications were imported into apparently simple and unambiguous suggestions, that an intelligent decision on them became almost impossible. At any rate, after six days of arduous debate, the Conference was persuaded that it could make no substantial progress along this line ; and determined to send this subject also to a Commission.

On the other hand, on a problem so complex as this, it may have seemed desirable to give an opportunity in general debate for all sections of the Conference to express their views. From this aspect, the procedure was fortunate enough. To have set up a Commission at the outset would pretty certainly have meant only a postponement of the evil day. A large

[1] See p. 119.

number of delegates had obviously come prepared to debate this question, and they were not inclined to practise the virtue of self-restraint.   When the question did finally reach the Commission stage, the Commission began its work possessing a reasonably full acquaintance with the attitude of the various groups and nationalities.

The Treaty had laid down, as one of the principles of an international industrial order, the limitation of hours of work to eight per day or forty-eight in the week.
The General The delegates, therefore, began their delibera-
Debate. tions on this subject with their respective Governments already committed in principle to the acceptance of this proposal.   But the acceptance of a proposal in principle, and the detailed elaboration of it into a legislative scheme, are two entirely different things ; though the Conference had reason to be grateful for the wisdom which included in the Treaty a definite declaration of principle.   Without the support of such a declaration, it is likely enough that, under the pressure of the necessity for making the adjustments appropriate to industries of all sizes, kinds, and conditions, the general principle would have been overborne and submerged.   As it was, the attempt to specify completely within the four corners of the Convention every circumstance which should be held to warrant some modification of its terms, broke down, and a different procedure was ultimately adopted.

The opening of the debate furnished a very fair example of the unexpected and unmerited troubles in which the Conference was apt to find itself.   Mr. Barnes, as has been recorded, put forward the suggestion that the draft Convention prepared by the Organising Committee should be taken as a basis of discussion : plainly intending no more than that the Conference should have a definite text to work upon, and not in any way implying that any specific proposal in the text should be accepted.   It happened that the Organising Committee had taken the view that the forty-eight-hour week, rather than the eight-hour day, was the more suitable principle on which to base the Convention.   The Labour delegates felt serious objection to this view, and suspected at once— though obviously nothing of the sort was intended—that the acceptance of the Committee's draft as a basis for discussion would commit them to accepting the forty-eight-hour week to the exclusion of the eight-hour day.   It took two days of argument and amendment before this quite unnecessary mystification was cleared away. In a monoglot Conference, accustomed to one form of Parliamentary procedure, the difficulty would probably have disappeared in ten minutes.

In the general confusion raised by this issue, the employers' group introduced a series of detailed amendments to the Organising Committee's draft, which amounted practically to a new Convention. It accepted, technically, the principle of a forty-eight-hour week, but it contemplated very large exceptions to and modifications of the general rule, and permitted a somewhat serious delay in bringing even the eviscerated Convention into operation. Naturally enough, the workers' representatives felt some alarm at the limitations which the employers placed on the application of the principle ; and on their behalf, M. Jouhaux brought forward, as an alternative, a very simple declaration that the eight-hour day and the forty-eight-hour week should be regarded as maxima.

These proposals had very little to do with Mr. Barnes' suggestion, which was ostensibly the subject of debate. But they served as texts for the further general discussion which followed the acceptance of the original resolution. The theme of the whole debate was the effect of the eight-hour day on production. The employers fought hard to abate or to delay the introduction of this universal limitation, until the present desperate state of Europe was remedied. The workers were persuaded that the line of remedy was not to maintain longer hours of work, but that economically, as well as physically and morally, the reform was urgent. The debate, for all its meandering, was at times really brilliant. The protagonists were two of the most forceful personalities of the Conference—the French representatives of the conflicting interests. M. Jouhaux's vigorous and tumultuous eloquence led the discussion to a consideration of the motives which were stirring the workers everywhere to demand opportunities for a more ample life than had hitherto been their portion. " De tous les points du monde, du nord au midi, de l'est à l'ouest, les voix fatiguées des travailleurs montent à l'horizon pour réclamer une place plus grande au soleil de la nature. . . . C'est à vous qu'il appartient, ici, dans la plénitude de votre responsabilité, de dire si vous ne voulez pas tenter loyalement l'effort nécessaire pour aboutir un résultat positif que nous cherchons tous. C'est dans cet esprit que nous avons redigé notre motion et nos amendements, c'est pour ces raisons que nous les exposons devant vous, et c'est également pour ces motifs que nous vous demandons d'y réfléchir profondément, en vous disant qu'il n'y a pas dans le monde que des intérêts arithmétiques, qu'il y a également des questions d'idéalisme, de moralité, qui guident les masses et qui sont les plus sûrs garants du développement ininterrompu du progrès social au bénéfice de tous." M. Guérin, a less passionate, but keener and subtler mind than M. Jouhaux, and with a greater power of incisive utterance, was content to recall to the Conference the cold facts of the world's condition. " Messieurs, il y a, en effet, des considérations morales ; et je suis d'accord avec M. Jouhaux pour dire que la vie ne se compose pas que d'intérêts arithmétiques. Mais elle ne se compose pas non plus seulement, d'intérêts arithmétiques et de considérations morales, elle se compose aussi des necessités de vivre." These elemental necessities of life were everywhere lacking throughout the world ; and until the fabric of civilization was secure against destruction through mere material privation, until especially the devastated regions of Europe were restored once more to their normal prosperity, the Conference should take no step which might diminish in the smallest way the production of those goods for want of which the world was in such straits. Nothing more interesting occurred during the whole Conference than this conflict of temperament, experience, and philosophy of life between the two French leaders.

Unfortunately, the remainder of the discussion was less pointed and vigorous, and hardly served to advance in any way the consideration of the question. There was, indeed, little more to be done in the way of general discussion. The issue had been set forth in an emphatic and unambiguous fashion ; it remained only to see whether any accommodation could be found of the two points of view. The successive declarations on either side—for at this stage the Government delegates had comparatively little to contribute, except occasional narratives of fact—brought no essential modification of the position. Hence it happened that, after some further days of fruitless rhetoric, the Conference was glad to surrender the question to the charge of a Commission, and await the outcome of its deliberations.

Ten sessions of the Conference, therefore, had been consumed in reaching the point at which it had established two

Commissions to deal with the first item on its agenda : one to examine the general question and draw out the terms of the main Convention, the second to propose the modifications appropriate to those countries whose situation required special treatment. It seemed, at the time, a small enough accomplishment, but, in fact, the Conference had now passed its most difficult period. It had explored its business, settled more or less comfortably into a definite order of procedure, learned something of the limits of its own possibilities, measured the strength of the opposing interests, and, in the light of its experience, had referred its most contentious business to a Commission, with the tacit understanding that if the Commission succeeded in reaching a reasonable measure of agreement the Conference would accept its findings.

Both Commissions were presided over by a British Chairman—the main Commission by a workers' representative, Mr. Tom Shaw, M.P. ; the Commission on the *The Com-* Special Countries by Mr. G. N. Barnes. *missions.* Throughout the Conference the British delegation—somewhat against its will—made rather a speciality of providing Chairmen for Commissions and Sub-Commissions. But in this case, as in most others, neither Commission had any cause to repent its choice. The patience and industry of both Chairmen, and their power of discovering the moment and the form of an acceptable solution, were of the greatest service. They had very difficult teams to drive, and, with less skilful handling, both Commissions might easily have failed to stay the course.

The main Commission started on its work, having before it the proposals of the Organising Committee and the amendments to it submitted by the three sections of the Conference. A great many questions of detail were necessarily discussed, but the most difficult decisions were on points of principle. The Commission had to determine, for example, whether it would attempt to regulate all types of industry, or exclude certain branches or forms ; whether it would prescribe an eight-hour day, or (in order to permit a week-end rest) a forty-eight-hour week ; and, if the latter, whether or not it would regulate the distribution of hours between the working days. On the first point, the Commission decided to treat each industry as a whole, so that a regulation drafted for any industry should cover workers of all grades and occupations within it, excepting only those who were engaged in a managerial or confidential capacity. It was determined also to bring all industries within the Convention, and to except only, on the ground of administrative difficulty, domestic industries. Even here, however, the Commission safeguarded the position as far as possible by confining " domestic industries " to those cases in which only members of the same family are employed. On the second, the formula of a forty-eight-hour week, with an eight-hour day, was adopted ; but in cases where, on one day a week, a shorter period is worked, the normal maximum of eight hours might be increased by not more than one hour.

More difficult decisions had to be taken on the question as to what exceptions to or temporary abrogations of the Convention might be permitted. Industries worked on a shift system were easily accommodated by extending the unit of calculation from one week to three. Again, in industries such as certain branches of railway work, where it is not easy to arrange for the uniform termination of work at a given hour, organisations of employers and workers were given power to arrange, with the sanction of the Government concerned, an extension of the daily maximum, provided that the prescribed weekly maximum was not exceeded. Cases of accident or of a breakdown of machinery were accepted readily enough as justifying a temporary extension of hours on occasions where that course was necessary to prevent serious interference with the ordinary work of the establishment. Again, there are some industries, such as the operation of blast furnaces, which are continuous in character, and therefore require to be carried on seven days a week. These, plainly, could not be brought under the forty-eight-hour limit without a large expansion in personnel. The Commission, therefore, accepted a fifty-six-hour week for these workers, and threw upon the national Governments the duty of providing by law the holidays necessary to compensate the workers for the loss of their weekly rest day.

All these special problems, of course, though they differed in detail, were marginal cases of the central problem of overtime : and it was this problem which presented the greatest difficulty. Evidently it was useless, from an international point of view, to make a Convention limiting hours of work and at the same time to leave it open to employers (or workers) to arrange for a substantial amount of overtime. The eight-hour day would be such only in name, and the only advantage of the nominal limitation would be that the workers might be able to claim a higher rate of pay for the additional hours. On the other hand, it was exceedingly difficult to define the circumstances in which overtime might be permitted, in a formula exact enough to be administratively practicable, and comprehensive enough to cover all legitimate cases. This was what the Organising Committee's draft Convention had attempted to do. It distinguished between various kinds of industries according to their liability to occasions for overtime, and tried to make appropriate assessments for each of these types. But when the Commission approached the consideration of this classification, it could neither accept it nor replace it by a better. Moreover, it was felt that to attempt quite rigid demarcations on the basis of the information at the disposal of the Conference, might easily produce an unworkable scheme. It was therefore resolved to proceed, meantime at all events, on a more flexible plan.

The Commission set itself first to secure an effective restriction of overtime to cases of proved necessity ; secondly, to make it economically disadvantageous to the employer, so that he should not be tempted to encourage it—though this process has the unfortunate consequence of making overtime more financially attractive to the workers ; and, thirdly, to provide as a safeguard against private collusion to evade the Convention the fullest publicity for any overtime arrangements. It discriminated therefore between two kinds of overtime, that which is permanently necessary—as, for instance, in the case of those workers whose duties require them to be in attendance before or after the main body of workers—door-keepers, watchmen, cleaners ; and the like— and that which is exceptional, as, for instance, in seasonal industries or industries liable to sudden pressure of work. Permanent exceptions in one case and temporary exceptions in the other may be made by the competent public authority, after consultation with the organisations of the employers and workers concerned, provided (a) that in every case the overtime rate of pay is at least 25 per cent above the normal rate ; and (b) that full information on every decision is conveyed to the International Labour Office, so that it may be at the disposal of all parties interested. The duty of sanctioning and of regulating overtime is therefore expressly laid on the public authority, and its action is doubly safeguarded : first, by economic considerations, and, secondly, by the fact that full information about it is accessible to all directly or indirectly concerned. The workers' representatives on the Commission wished to fix an upper limit beyond which the public authority might not go ; the employers' to leave all matters relating to rate of pay for overtime to the organisations concerned. But finally, by a majority in each case, the Commission took its course between both these proposals ; it imposed no limit, but it did impose a constitutional financial safeguard.

These were the main provisions of the general Convention as they were framed by the Commission, and as they finally passed the Conference. They differ considerably from all the documents on which the Commission based its work, but they embodied a position which it was possible for all parties to support. The employers had secured a certain amount of elasticity in arrangements ; the workers had secured that that amount could not for long be so great as to overthrow the principle of the eight-hour day.

The report of the Commission had a tolerably easy passage through the Conference itself. One minor amendment was introduced ; and a resolute attempt was made by the workers' delegates to secure an addition to the Convention, providing that in cases where, as a result of the Convention, hours of work were shortened, no decrease in wages should ensue. This last consideration, however, since it dealt with a question of wages rather than of hours, could not properly become part of the Convention ; and the workers were content, finally, to secure the unanimous assent of the Conference to a statement of its hope that wages would not be adversely affected. Other amendments were brought forward of some significance. One, for instance, proposed to extend the Convention to domestic industries ; another to modify the terms of the clause relating to continuous shift industries. But the Conference, though well enough aware of these problems, and anxious to give some further attention to them at a subsequent meeting when fuller information was available, was decisively of opinion that no practicable step could be taken on the present occasion.

After considerable discussion, therefore, but without a single substantial alteration, the Conference accepted the finding of the Commission. Clause by clause went through with varying, but mostly with large, majorities, and on the final vote for the acceptance of the Convention as a whole only one dissentient vote was recorded. No section, of course, had succeeded in getting its full programme. All sections had some hesitation about particular provisions, and reserved to themselves the right to bring up at a later meeting proposals for revision. But, on the whole, a real piece of legislation had been accomplished ; and all sections of the Conference were prepared to welcome the Convention as a happy accomplishment of its most testing duty.

Mr. Barnes' Commission on Special Countries had, on the whole, a less controversial experience ; but it is probable that the results of its deliberations will initiate *The Commission on Special Countries.* more profound changes in the conditions of life of many millions of workers than any other act of the Conference. The crowded countries of the Orient fell within the purview of the Commission ; and if, as there is reason to believe, its recommendations become effective, a very great and humane movement in the industry of the East will have been inaugurated. The whole problem is certainly one of the greatest difficulty. Industrial practices in the East are the outcome of a social tradition very different from that of Europe and the West ; and it would be profoundly dangerous to break down Eastern customs and standards without replacing them by others equally substantial and intelligible to the Eastern mind. Nevertheless, some definite evils admittedly exist which are capable of slow and gradual remedy. And it was with these points that the Commission and the Conference were chiefly concerned.

Certain minor points were referred to this Commission, and disposed of without difficulty. Greece and Roumania requested permission to delay for a short time the application of the provisions of the main Convention, on the ground, in the former case, of the disorganisation of its administrative system in the new territories ; in the latter, of the complete lack of machinery in the country, as the result of the ravages of war. Both of these applications were approved. In the cases of Tropical America and of South Africa no modification of the main Convention was found to be necessary. China, Persia, and Siam presented rather greater difficulty. Industry in these countries, as over the greater part of the East, is still primitive, and largely in the domestic stage. The Governments are also administratively weak, and without experience in factory legislation. On the other hand, the industrialization of these countries is proceeding apace.

China has some well-equipped cotton mills, which compete with Japanese and Indian factories ; and if these countries were to be asked to impose restrictions on their hours of work, it seemed desirable that some similar provision should be made in the case of China.   In all three cases the Commission recommended that the Governments should be asked to adhere to the principle of the protection of Labour by factory legislation and to report to the next Conference on the measures by which it was proposed to bring that principle into operation.   It was suggested for the consideration of the Chinese Government that it might adopt a Convention embodying the principle of a ten-hour day or a sixty-hour week for adult factory [1] workers, and an eight-hour day or a forty-eight hour week for employed persons under fifteen years of age, and recognizing also the principle of a weekly rest day.

In India, again, only a very small proportion of the population is engaged in organised industry, and even in such *India.* industry conditions and habits of work differ profoundly from those which obtain in the West.   Nevertheless here, as in China, industrial development is rapid.   Textile industries, railway and engineering works, mines and iron works, all exist on a considerable scale.   Moreover, India has had experience of three well-administered factory laws—each marking a distinct advance on its predecessor.   But the law covers practically only textile and certain branches of railway work, and is confined to establishments in which at least fifty persons are employed, though in cases where abuses are suspected it is possible to bring under the scope of the law establishments employing twenty persons.

The representatives of the Government of India were somewhat unwilling that the Commission should make any substantial recommendations in the case of India.   They indicated that the main difficulty in the way of an immediate enlargement of the Factory Acts—and especially of any redrafting of the definition of a " factory " so as to bring within the Acts smaller establishments than those now affected by it— was the complete absence of information as to the smaller industries of India.   The Government, therefore, was quite unable to measure the administrative responsibilities which

[1] A " factory," in this instance, was to be defined as an establishment employing over one hundred persons.

6

an extension of the Acts would require it to undertake. It was at the moment engaged on an enquiry on this point ; and it desired that the Conference should delay the consideration of the Indian position until the results were available, and the Government had had time to submit its proposals.

The Commission, however, was not unsympathetic to the plea of the Indian Labour delegate that the Government would be nothing the worse for a little stimulation ; and, especially in view of the suggestions which it was making to other Oriental countries, it thought it well to take a larger view of its duties than was contemplated by the Government spokesmen. It therefore embodied in the Convention a definite prescription with regard to India : that in all industries under the Factory Acts, and also in mines (at present quite unprotected), and in specified branches of railway work, the principle of a sixty-hour week should be brought into operation. It added also three forcible and urgent recommendations : (1) that in mines the Government should at once try to effect a reduction to fifty-four hours a week, or even lower ; (2) that the definition of a "factory" should be revised, so as to bring within the range of the Acts smaller establishments than those employing fifty persons ; and (3) that the researches at present in progress should be expedited, so that at the earliest possible date the Government of India might be able to lay before the Conference its proposals for a still further extension of labour protection. The Labour delegate urged both to the Commission and to the Conference the desirability of giving further protection to women workers ; but he was content to accept the Convention and the Recommendations which were drafted, as at least a substantial instalment of reform.

The problem of Japan was at once the most interesting and the most difficult. Industrial development in that country is proceeding at a much greater rate than elsewhere in the East, though it is superimposed upon a somewhat primitive economic organisation. The only Factory Act in Japan applies to women and children. For these workers a maximum working day of thirteen hours is established ; and in addition to this extravagantly long day a liberal amount of overtime is permitted. Work is carried on as a rule seven days a week. Custom, it is true, is better than the law ; and somewhat shorter hours (though still very long, and subject to increase by overtime)

Japan.

are the usual practice. The Japanese delegates agreed that in all the main industries of Japan, except in heavy metal works, a twelve-hour day was the normal rule. But no legal protection of any sort is extended to male operatives ; and even in the case of women and children the Act covers only factories employing fifteen persons or more ; so that in a country where domestic industry is still prevalent, a great part, probably the majority, of women workers are not affected by it.

Two things were clear to the Commission : first, that it was imperative to bring about, at the earliest possible date, a very great change in Japanese conditions ; and, second, that Japan could not at one step move from its existing level to the full acceptance of the main Convention. The latter point, however, was warmly contested by the Japanese Labour delegate. He desired that Japan should be treated on exactly the same footing as the countries of Europe and America. Japan, he argued, aspired to be regarded as one of the chief industrial powers of the world ; the Government, therefore, should be prepared and enjoined to accept responsibilities for the regulation of industry commensurate with the national ambition. On the other hand, he believed that neither climatically nor technically was it impossible for Japanese industry at once to be reorganised in conformity to Western standards. The proof of it was in the fact that already several labour unions had succeeded in establishing the principle of the eight-hour day.[1] The issue thus raised was debated both in the Commission and in the Conference. The Commission was decisively on the side of temporary modifications of the Convention, but in the Conference itself the Labour group, reinforced by a considerable number of Government votes, and by a few employers, almost succeeded in carrying their case. Forty-five voted for modifications, forty-two against.[2]

The main question having been determined, no great difficulty was experienced in deciding upon the appropriate provisions. The Japanese Government had declared " its intention to accelerate the unqualified adoption of the eight-hour rule in harmony with the general trend of the world." The

[1] It was found, however, that this did not mean the observance of the eight-hour day in practice. All that was implied is that eight hours is taken as the basic day. The additional hours which are invariably worked count as overtime.

[2] See p. 13.

delegates of both the Government and the employers were prepared with a programme of very rapid and significant improvement ; which, with a few changes, the Commission and the Conference were able cordially to accept. A most gratifying and unexpected ending to a long discussion was the undertaking of the representative of the Japanese employers, given spontaneously and with evident sincerity, that, though he had failed to obtain all the concessions which he desired, he and his fellow-employers would press on the Government the complete acceptance of the terms which had been agreed upon, and give every assistance in their administration.

These terms propose a great and universal reduction of hours. Factory Acts are to apply to all establishments employing at least ten persons ; and their provisions are to extend to male workers as well as to women and children. Children under fifteen (after 1925, under sixteen) must not be employed for more than forty-eight hours in the week. The same limit is to apply to the coal-mining industry. Most other industries are to work a maximum day of nine and a half hours or fifty-seven hours in the week. The raw silk industry alone (but not silk manufacture) may have its maxima fixed at ten and sixty hours respectively. Overtime in all cases is to be permitted and regulated in the manner laid down in the main Convention. The observance of a weekly day of rest is to be made universal. And this measure of improvement, substantial though it is, is regarded as transitional, so that, after the experience gained by the application of these regulations, Japan may be able to make further advance at an early date. It will be found that in other matters the Conference, with the consent and approval of the representatives of the Japanese Government, has asked that Government to effect changes almost as great as those prescribed in relation to hours of work. No doubt changes would have occurred in Japanese industry in any case. But the Conference, at the lowest estimate, has brought powerful support to the reforming forces in Japan. It threw into relief the contrast between Japanese and Western conditions, and gave a clear leading as to the methods by which the most urgent changes should be accomplished. Whatever is done in Japan will be done in full view of the organised interests of the rest of the world ; and it will not be easy for Japan to resist the pressure of informed Western opinion.

It is not too much to believe that as the result of the Conference the inevitable changes in Japan will come more speedily,
more securely, and with less opposition than would otherwise
have been possible.

One further point deserves to be noted.   Much of the discussion in this Commission was occupied with the comparison
of standards in different Oriental countries, and with the
attempt to reach mutual adjustment.   Under the influence
of the general spirit of the Conference the tendency was to
adjust on the higher levels.   Thus, e.g. the South African
delegates were anxious that the main Convention, without
modification, should apply to the industries of their country.
South African coal, however, competes with Indian coal for
certain Eastern markets, and the conditions of coal production are much the same in both countries.   They therefore
made it clear that it might be impossible for South Africa
to accept a restriction from which India was exempt.   Hence
the decision of the Commission (accepted by the representatives of the Government of India), first, to include coal-mining
in the Convention relating to India ; and, secondly, to urge the
Government to improve on the standard prescribed there.
Similar adjustments were attempted between India and
Japan and between Japan and China.

Without an International Conference it is hardly likely
that negotiations like these would readily have been undertaken : and even if that had been done, it would have been
easy and natural to make the adjustments on a lower level
than that which was agreed at Washington.   For there
the discussion related not solely to the affairs of any two
countries, but to the progress which it was possible for these
countries to make in conformity with tendencies which were
at work throughout the whole of civilization.   Beneath the
consideration of any particular problem there lay the desire
to effect, not only an adjustment, but the largest advance
which was seriously possible.

Chapter VII

UNEMPLOYMENT

THE second subject which the Conference had to consider was the prevention of or provision against unemployment. The Conference referred the subject in the first instance to a large Commission of thirty members, over which M. Max Lazard, a French Government delegate, was chosen to preside. That Commission in turn divided itself into three Sub-Commissions. The first [1] considered questions relating to the systematic observation and prevention of unemployment ; the second, [2] questions relating to the protection of the unemployed, especially by the organisation of employment exchanges and insurance services ; the third, [3] questions relating to the migration of workers from one country to another. The whole Commission examined the reports of the Sub-Commissions, amended and correlated them, and brought to the full Conference a Report containing a series of draft Conventions, Recommendations, and Resolutions. These were fully and carefully discussed by the Conference, amended in some important particulars, and finally adopted by the necessary majority. The proceedings both in the Commission and in the Conference were protracted and intricate. But since, in the end, both assemblies were able to make their decisions with a great measure of unanimity, it is necessary to call attention only to the most significant points of the discussions.

The Commission.

Perhaps the most notable feature of the consideration of this problem was the expansion of the area of discussion. In particular, two important matters were raised in connexion with it, both of which were discussed, and one of which became the subject of legislation.

The Italian Labour Delegate, Signor Gino Baldesi, fertile

[1] Chairman, M. Lazard.
[2] Chairman, Mr. J. F. G. Price (Great Britain).
[3] Chairman, the Viscount de Eza (Spain).

here as everywhere in ideas and arguments, contended that one important cause of unemployment was the unequal distribution of raw materials throughout the world, and the difficulties in their transport from the country of origin to the country of manufacture. He therefore suggested that the Conference (since the matter was not obviously one within its own competence) should invite the attention of the League of Nations to this problem, and request the initiation of organised study of it. The support for this proposal in debate came mainly from the Labour group, but the vote showed a remarkably even division of opinion in all three sections of the Conference. The main argument against Signor Baldesi's view was simply the consideration that at the moment not very much could be hoped for from the course which he proposed. The countries which were fortunate enough to be rich in materials, were not likely willingly to accept any scheme for their easy redistribution ; and it was unwise to invite the League, thus early in its career, to court a certain failure. The subject must necessarily recur, for it is plainly one of fundamental importance. But for this Conference it was disposed of by the narrow rejection of the motion by forty-three votes to forty.

A second relevant, but partially unforeseen, point which fell to be considered was the establishment of the principle of reciprocity in the treatment of workers *Reciprocity.* who had migrated from one State to another. The end which it was intended to secure by this principle was that workers who settle in another country than that of their birth, should be admitted to all the protection against industrial misfortune which their adopted country affords to its own citizens.

The point arose first in connexion with the organisation of public systems of insurance against unemployment. One of the minor defects of all such systems at present is that an emigrant worker cannot transfer to his new country the benefits which had accrued to him under his national system. The Commission, therefore, suggested to the Conference, and the Conference accepted without demur, the insertion of a clause in the Convention dealing with Unemployment, providing that states which had established national systems of insurance against unemployment should make arrangements whereby, under terms and conditions agreed upon by the Governments concerned, a worker belonging to one State, but employed in the territory of another, should be admitted by the latter to the same rates of benefit as obtained in the case of its own nationals. No objection could be taken to this proposal. It was a concrete and appropriate international enactment, designed to remedy a defect in the existing provision against unemployment, and as such directly within the competence of the Conference. The obligation which it seeks to impose on the ratifying States is simply that they should agree to admit each other's citizens to benefits, and themselves work out the terms of the adjustments, financial and other, required by the transfer of a claim from one State to another.

But the assertion of the general principle of reciprocity, apart from this particular embodiment of it, evidently raises questions of a much more complex character. The Commission, with only one dissentient, invited the Conference to enact a Convention providing for the reciprocal admission by each State of workers belonging to another, " to the benefits of the laws and regulations bearing on labour protection, as well as to the right of lawful organisation." The obvious meaning of the Convention as thus drafted was to pledge every ratifying State, under conditions of reciprocal treatment, to admit workers, still subject to another Government, to all the privileges in industrial matters conferred upon its own members. The principle is certainly unexceptionable, but its application in this general form would be difficult. One of the delegates of the Swiss Government, though approving the aim of the Convention, gave some pertinent examples of the difficulties which would arise. The Swiss factory law, for example, prescribes that an employer cannot cancel his contract with an employé on the ground that the latter has been conscripted : and during a certain part of his military service the worker is entitled to receive his wages. The whole position on which these benefits are founded would clearly be changed if the worker were subject to the call, not of the Swiss Government, but of some other.

It is, indeed, hard to resist the conclusion that a Convention conceived in so vague and general a form as this could achieve little real success. Much more precise definition is required as to the extent of the reciprocal obligations, and as to the rights and privileges which can thus be made accessible to extra-national workers. At the same time it is clear —as the single example of unemployment insurance showed—

that there is here a subject pre-eminently suited both for international discussion and for national negotiation.

The Swiss delegation therefore chose what was probably the best course in asking the Conference to refer the proposed Convention to the International Labour Office for examination and report to a later Conference. They were able to plead, most relevantly and forcibly, that since the general question of reciprocity of treatment had not been on the agenda of the Conference, no preliminary work had been done upon it, and no Government had been able to instruct its delegates. The Conference could not legislate wisely ; and in any case had no real mandate to legislate at all. The whole delegation of great Britain supported the Swiss contention ; and it plainly commanded the assent of the more constitutionally minded Members of the Conference. But it was defeated by forty-seven votes to twenty-six.

The discussion, however, did not entirely fail of its purpose. The Conference decided not to accept the Convention as drafted by the Commission, but to substitute for it a more precisely-worded Recommendation,[1] and to defer the framing of a Convention until the experience of the working of the Recommendation was available for its guidance.

The further transactions of the Conference in relation to unemployment occasioned less acute controversy. One

Further enactments.

(a) Assembly of information.

primary requisite of any intelligent handling of the situation is the collection of all the data required for an authoritative study of it. The investigations of the Organising Committee had shown that, while many countries had readily available the information necessary for the examination of the problems from a national point of view, such was not universally the case, and no satisfactory provision existed anywhere for considering the larger aspects of the problem. It is plainly the business of the International Labour Office to investigate the international issues of unemployment ; and this requires that the information should be assembled on a more or less uniform plan. The Conference, therefore, accepted the proposal of the Commission that the Convention should impose on Members the duty to furnish to the Office at short intervals " all the available information, statistical and otherwise, concerning unemployment, including reports

[1] See Appendix, p. 168.

on measures taken or contemplated to combat unemployment." It also instructed the Office to establish an international Commission, which should make recommendations as to the methods by which each State could best collect the information in the form most serviceable for the purposes of comparative study.

Employment Exchanges are established in most countries to facilitate the transfer of workers from one post to another. The Conference decided that all Members (b) *Employment Exchanges.* should be asked to equip themselves with such a system of exchanges, and that the International Office should co-ordinate the operation of the national systems, so that each might know the needs and possibilities of the others. The Convention prescribes that the system should be one of free public exchanges, and that the operations of the exchanges should be supervised (apparently on the model of the British local advisory committees) by committees of employers and workers. Where both public and private free exchanges exist, these should be integrated into a single system. Two further Recommendations were passed, dealing with the same problem. States in which private profit-making exchanges do not exist are recommended to prohibit their institution ; States in which they do exist are recommended to permit them only under licence, and, as soon as possible, to abolish them. Again it is recommended that the recruiting of bodies of workers in one State for employment in another should be permitted only after agreement between the countries interested, and after consultation with the employers and workers in the industries concerned.

No serious difficulty was raised on any of these points, though some Members of the Conference, who agreed as to the desirability of pressing for the universal establishment of free public exchanges, were doubtful as to the propriety of the Conference's action in specifying what the exact mode of organisation should be.

The view which the Commission took on this subject, and the subsequent action of the Conference upon it, have already been noted. The only provision which was (c) *Insurance.* embodied in Convention form was the suggestion that States in which systems of unemployment insurance existed, should make arrangements for such a transfer of benefits as would enable a worker who had passed from one State to another to be admitted to the full benefits obtainable in the State in which he was employed. A further Recommendation was added that Members which had not yet adopted a system of unemployment insurance should do so either on the British pattern of a State scheme, or on the Ghent system of grants from public funds to associations which pay benefits to unemployed members. The Commission suggested that after some experience of the working of both schemes, it might be possible at a later Conference to draft a Convention on the matter.

It is evident from the terms of the Conventions and Recommendations thus enacted that the Conference, very appropriately, was occupied throughout its discussion predominantly with the international aspects of the provision against unemployment. Its conclusions, too, as one Labour delegate complained, were directed more towards methods of cure than methods of prevention.

It is no doubt significant of the limitations of international preventive action that the only Recommendation dealing directly with prevention should have prescribed a purely domestic remedy. It proposes a measure (d) *Reserva-* which has long been urged by all competent *tion of* authorities on the subject, that in every state *public works.* the larger foreseeable undertakings of public authorities should be reserved for those periods in which a cyclical depression of trade is seen to be impending ; so that the demand for labour should be maintained at a more nearly uniform level than would otherwise be the case.

In line with the prevailing interest of the Conference, two further resolutions of instruction to the International Labour Office were passed. The first advocated the creation of a special section of the Office to study the problems arising from the migration of workers. The second asked for the appointment of an international Commission to report to the Conference on the measures which might be adopted to control the migration of workers, and to protect the interests of emigrants in the country of their adoption. The Conference in accepting the second resolution added an interesting proviso—that the representatives of European States on the international Commission should not constitute more than half its number. There was plainly marked here the division of interest between the older countries, which would be glad to retain at home as many of their workers as possible, and the new countries, which wished to attract a vigorous stock of settlers. The same division had occurred on the question of the distribution of raw materials ; and during the Conference it showed itself in other ways. It is not the least interesting of the lines of demarcation in the Conference, and may well be not the least troublesome to negotiate.

Chapter VIII

THE EMPLOYMENT OF WOMEN

BESIDES the regulation of hours of work and the consideration of unemployment, the agenda of the Conference contained three further items: relating to the employment of women, the employment of children, and the universal adoption of the Berne Convention of 1906 prohibiting the use of white *The Berne* phosphorus in the manufacture of matches. *Convention of* Most States had already given their adherence *of* 1906. to the latter Convention ; and at the Conference, the representatives of almost every State which had not yet acceded, intimated the intention of their Governments to do so. This subject, therefore, called for no detailed consideration.

The two remaining items were referred to Commissions by the usual procedure. Three Commissions were appointed : one to deal specially with children's employment,[1] the second to deal with certain aspects of the employment of women, the third to deal with the employment of both women and children in dangerous or unhealthy processes.

The report of the third Commission,[2] although it issued in important Recommendations, requires very brief notice. The whole field is one which is eminently *Dangerous* suited for international action. Indeed, many *or unhealthy* of its problems, e.g., those connected with the *processes.* transmission of diseases, cannot be effectively solved except through such action. No opposition was raised from any section of the Conference to any of the proposals of the Commission. The sole amendment which was made was in the form of an addition.

The Commission in its deliberations found that a very large area of investigation had been opened to it, and that it could do no more than select a few typical subjects. Even on these it was impossible to proceed very far ; and with

[1] See next chapter, p. 91.
[2] The Chairman was Dr. T. M. Legge (Great Britain).

regard to most of them the Commission were content to lay down lines of research to be pursued by the International Labour Office, with a view to definite enactments at succeeding Conferences.[1] It suggested, moreover, that the Conference should recommend to all Members of the Labour Organisation the establishment, not only of a system of factory inspection, but of a Government industrial health service which might keep in touch with the international Office. This Recommendation, therefore, was duly passed by the Conference.

Two further matters became the subject of enactments by the Conference. The most widely spread danger to women and young persons in industry is that of infection with lead poisoning. The Commission felt sufficiently sure of its data on this point to bring before the Conference a series of detailed proposals which could be translated into legislation. These were embodied, in the first instance, in a Recommendation ; so that after some experience of their working they may be given, at a later Conference, the status of a Convention. It is proposed entirely to exclude women and young persons from employment in certain specified dangerous processes ; and to impose restrictions and conditions upon their employment in any process involving the use of lead compounds.[2] A Recommendation was also passed on the prevention of anthrax. It is suggested that arrangements should be made for the treatment of wool infected with anthrax spores, preferably in the country of export, or if that is impracticable, at the port of entry in the country receiving the wool.

The Commission on the Employment of Women[3] had to deal with two problems : the employment of women during the night, and the employment of women before and after childbirth. The way for the consideration of the first topic had been prepared by the Berne Convention of 1906, to which many important industrial States had adhered. The text of that Convention was taken as a basis for discussion and

The Employ-
ment of
women :
(a) During
the night.

---

[1] It was quite clear that if the Office were effectively to undertake the duties assigned to it, it would be necessary to constitute a health section. This, as has been noted (p. 58), was formally decided upon by the Governing Body at its meeting in March, 1920.

[2] See p. 178.

[3] Chairman, Miss Constance Smith (Great Britain).

amendment, especially in the light of the prolonged experience in all belligerent countries of the effects of the night work of women during the war. It was significant of the lessons conveyed by that experience that the main effort of the Commission was directed to strengthening the restrictions imposed by the Berne Convention.

The fundamental principle which was adopted was the prohibition of the employment of women in all industrial occupations during at least eleven consecutive hours in the night, including the period from ten p.m. to five a.m. The Berne Convention had limited the application of the prohibition to establishments in which at least ten persons were engaged. The Commission withdrew that limitation. Experience had proved that the worst offenders were just such small establishments as had hitherto been excepted ; and it was resolved that the prohibition should apply universally to all industry other than purely domestic. The only modifications permitted concern (1) industries in which the materials treated are subject to rapid deterioration, in which case the necessary labour may be employed at night so far as is necessary to avoid certain loss ; and (2) industries which are subject to great seasonal fluctuation or other pressure in which cases the " night " period may be reduced, on sixty days of the year, to ten hours.

The difficulty of the application of the Convention to Oriental countries does not seem to have been severely felt. The Japanese representatives showed an honourable desire to expedite the process of its adoption ; and indicated the intention of their Government fully to observe its provisions. To meet the circumstances of other Eastern countries, especially of India, a special clause was inserted providing for the suspension of the Convention in any industrial undertaking except factories as defined by the national law. The effect, as regards India, is to bring under the Convention all establishments employing over fifty persons, or, if the factory law is amended in accordance with the urgent desire of the Conference, all establishments employing over twenty persons.

The only point which gave rise to a serious divergence of view was raised by the employment of women in industries which work in shifts of eight hours. The definite exclusion of women from employment between ten p.m. and five a.m. leaves only seventeen hours in the day when their employment is possible. To work two shifts in this space of seventeen hours requires either the reduction of the rest period within each shift to half an hour, or, if an hour's rest is granted, the reduction of the effective hours of work to seven and a half. When the Berne Convention was drafted few women were employed in industries of this character ; and the problem did not arise in any serious form.   In the face of this situation two contrary courses were urged.   The employers, through M. Guérin, proposed that where two shifts are worked, women should be permitted to work between either four a.m and ten p.m., or between five a.m and eleven p.m., thereby setting free an additional hour in the day.   On the other hand, the workers were disposed to suggest that the closed period should extend until six a.m.   Their contention was that the Conference had no other duty than to lay down the limits which it regarded as desirable.   It was the business of the industrial interests concerned to work out, within those limits, the arrangements which best suited their circumstances.   The Italian representatives were able to report that in their country the prohibition of women's employment between ten p.m. and six a.m. had been successfully carried through—the shift industries working nominally seven and a half hours, but effectively only seven.   In Norway the prohibition extends from nine p.m. till six a.m.—apparently without serious difficulty.   The Commission rejected both alternatives ; and when they were carried to the Conference itself, the Conference accepted the findings of the Commission.   The workers' amendment attracted more support than that of the employers.   The vote in the former case was forty-six to twenty-four, in the latter fifty-eight to sixteen.   This special difficulty having been settled the Convention as a whole was carried by a unanimous vote of the Conference.

The second aspect of women's employment—its regulation before and after childbirth—was the subject of one of the

(b) Before and after childbirth. most interesting debates in the Conference and of an important enactment.   Most countries have some legislation dealing with this problem but a study of the existing practice in the different States reveals a great diversity of method.   The one principle which is clearly discoverable is the necessity for some exclusion of women from employment immediately after confinement ; and there has been in the past decade an increasing assumption by public authorities

of the responsibility for providing some maintenance during the period of exclusion. But the period of exclusion and the range of employments covered by it, the amount and kind of the maintenance, vary greatly in different countries. South Africa, e.g., enforces an abstention of twelve weeks—four weeks before and eight weeks after the date of birth. Great Britain, Italy, and Denmark, on the other hand, prescribe an abstention of four weeks after confinement ; and in the case of the two latter countries the period may be shortened on a medical certificate of fitness. Again, in Great Britain the prohibition extends only to industrial employments ; in Belgium it covers not only factories and workshops, but mines, commercial establishments, restaurants, and offices attached to almost every kind of undertaking. In some countries there is provided either a compulsory or an optional period of rest before confinement, the latter being secured by the granting of a civil right to a woman to claim reinstatement after leaving her work within a certain period before childbirth, either on a medical certificate or without notice. Again, in most highly industrialized States some form of maternity benefit is established. Sometimes, as in Great Britain, it has no special connexion with the compulsory rest period, but is part of a general system of sickness insurance ; sometimes it is a specially organised service. The rates and benefits are similarly varied—in some cases a fixed uniform rate is paid, in others a proportion of wages. In some countries free attendance by a doctor or midwife is provided ; in others no such arrangement obtains. And inevitably, in dealing with a problem like this, where there are considerable opportunities for evasion, especially in connexion with the pre-natal period of rest, the variety of administrative methods is great.

Nevertheless, as has been noted, from all this diversity one or two common features emerge. Most civilized States have imposed a restriction on employment after child-birth ; and a period of four weeks seems everywhere to be acceptable as a minimum. Most States again appear to be prepared to accept some responsibility for granting main-enance. These two facts were therefore available as a foundation for an International Convention.

The Commission on women's employment in its preliminary survey of the field found itself able to agree without much difficulty on certain points of principle ; and it is noteworthy

7

that, from the outset, these embodied a standard of protective legislation considerably in advance of the practice of most countries. The points were : (1) that the Convention should cover only industrial employment ; (2) that the period of exclusion after childbirth should be six weeks ; (3) that a woman should have the right, if she chose to exercise it, of leaving her employment for some period in advance of the confinement ; and (4) that during the whole of her period of absence there should be secured to herself and her child full maintenance and free medical attendance.

The main difference of view arose in connexion with the third of these points. A majority of the Commission decided that the optional ante-natal rest period should extend to six weeks ; and proposed that a woman should be qualified for rest and benefit after the issue of a certificate by her medical adviser that her confinement would probably take place within six weeks. If it should happen that the doctor's estimate was wrong, and the confinement did not take place until after the anticipated date, the woman's right to benefit during the whole of her certified period of absence would remain unimpaired. The employer's group strongly resisted these proposals ; and urged the reduction of the ante-natal rest period to four weeks. On the other hand, the workers' group were equally opposed to a clause suggested by the practice of several European countries, and approved by a majority of the Commission, that after her return to work, a nursing mother should be allowed to leave her occupation for half an hour twice a day in order to feed her child. The ground of the objection was that it seemed to attach some kind of sanction to a system under which a woman's care of her child was subordinate to her industrial obligations. The Commission also discussed the possibility of fixing a uniform method for the payment of benefits, and a formula for the calculation of the amount of benefit. But no decision on either of these points appeared to be practicable. It was therefore determined to allow the method to be either direct payment by the State, or a system of public insurance and to prescribe no other rule as to amount than that the Government should order such a rate of benefit as to provide adequate maintenance for mother and child.

When the Report came before the Conference, the main provisions were accepted without question—six weeks exclusion after childbirth, some period of pre-natal rest and the right to maintenance and medical benefit. The discussion was concerned chiefly with the three points of comparative detail which had engaged the attention of the Commission. On none of these points was the decision of the Commission reversed ; but in another respect the Convention received an important amendment.

The greater part of the debate was occupied with the employers' amendment. The case for the reduction of the ante-natal rest period was presented by the Swedish and British employers, supported by a Swedish Government delegate. The Commission's decision was defended by Miss Mary MacArthur of Great Britain, supported by several of her Labour colleagues, and by the Government delegates of Norway and Italy. The issue was never seriously in doubt. The employers made the tactical mistake of contending that there was no advantage to the health of the expectant mother in extending her period of rest before childbirth—a position which exposed them to a vigorous *argumentum ad feminam* from Miss MacArthur. Her suggestion that the wives of employers in similar circumstances should profit by this expert medical advice and take employment in factories was as clear an *ignoratio* as arguments of the sort usually are ; but it was good debating, and left the opposition with no very effective answer. Indolence, at that period, she agreed, was bad for a woman ; but a working woman, even out of the factory, had small temptation to that indulgence, and a full six weeks of preparation for the coming of her child, in circumstances where she was assured of decent maintenance, was a far more profitable investment to the community than the extra time in the factory could ever be.

The workers' amendment to delete the clause relating to nursing mothers was defeated by fifty-four votes to twenty-nine. Unfortunately no debate was possible on the amendment ; but it is unlikely that the result would have been affected. The Commission had felt that the point deserved further consideration, and on its suggestion the Conference agreed that all participating Governments should be asked to consider the possibility of a longer continuance of post-natal benefits than was prescribed in the Convention, so that a working mother should be enabled to remain with her child. Unquestionably, such a system would offer much greater social advantages than one which restricts in any way the mother's access to her child. But the Convention does not bring such a system into being ; indeed, it almost postulates its non-existence. And, after the Conference's recognition of the principle at stake, the objection to safeguarding within the existing system the mother's right to care for her child, wears a certain air of doctrinaire intransigeance which contrasts strikingly with the detailed, vivid, and practical knowledge of working conditions which characterized most of the utterances of the Labour delegates.

Against the criticisms of both minorities, therefore, the Conference sustained the proposals of the Commission. But one important and unexpected change was made.[1]   On the proposal of the delegates of the Spanish Government, and almost without discussion, the Convention was applied to commerce as well as to industry.   Evidently there is a strong case for such an extension.   As M. Jouhaux pointed out, the number of women employed in commerce greatly exceeds the number employed in industry ; and there can hardly be any more disadvantageous occupation for a woman at a late stage of pregnancy than one which demands many hours of continuous standing or walking.   Nevertheless, it was somewhat disconcerting to find that a decision on an important point of principle could be taken with little discussion, and against the direct statement of the Commission which reported on the question, that the materials for a study of the application of the Convention to commerce had not been assembled.   It was obvious enough from the Chairman's observations—at this session Mr. Barnes— that he did not grasp the effect of the proposal ; and the brief debate showed that several members of the Conferences shared his uncertainty.   It was evidently one of the occasions on which the polyglot character of the Conference made it difficult for one section to interpret precisely the desire of another group.   But, whatever the reasons, this amendment was carried by thirty-seven to thirty-one; so that the provisions of this Convention alone of all those passed at Washington[2] affect other than industrial occupations.

No special clause was inserted in the Convention relating

[1] It should, perhaps, be recorded that on the motion of M. Jouhaux, an amendment was passed placing the responsibility for the payment of the benefits on the Governments of the ratifying States.   But since, constitutionally, the responsibility for securing the carrying out of the provisions of a Convention can rest nowhere but on the Governments, the purpose of the amendment is far from clear.

[2] Except, of course, those relating to unemployment.

to its application in Oriental countries. The Japanese Government delegates favoured the employers' amendment, but appeared to be prepared to accept this Convention along with that regulating the employment of women during the night. It was assumed, however—no doubt, justifiably— that the Government of India would not ratify the Convention ; and in view of that probability, a special resolution was passed requesting that Government to report to a later Conference on its proposals for dealing with this subject.

Two points in this debate are, perhaps, worthy of note. The first is the example of the misadventures to which the Conference is exposed, afforded by the resolu-

Comments. tion to apply the Convention to commerce as well as to industry. Whatever be the opinion as to the merits of the decision, it can hardly be regarded otherwise than as a misfortune that so important an issue should have been settled without adequate study or discussion. The standing orders of the Conference are designed to protect it against such a contingency. Notice of all amendments of substance must be given twenty-four hours in advance, so that they may be circulated to members of the Conference. The Chairman of the Conference has power to accept without notice, from the floor of the house, only minor amendments. In this instance the requisite notice was given ; but the implications of it clearly escaped the attention of the delegates. The decision on the first vote was in favour of the amendment, on the second against it ; and, finally, when a good deal of confusion had arisen, the first decision was reaffirmed by a formal record vote. Probably if the motion had been debated in detail it could hardly have succeeded. But the Conference, at this stage, was severely pressed for time, and the opportunity could not easily be given. It is unlikely that any serious difficulty will arise over this particular decision, but it is of first-rate importance that the Conference in future should be saved from hurrying to vote on matters of principle without much more careful preparation. The true moral is that the Conference should not be asked to attempt so much as on this occasion in the course of a single meeting.

A much more significant matter, however, is the disposition shown both by the Commission and the Conference to set the level of its enactments by the best available practice rather than by the lowest. Reference has already been made to the fear that the Conference might be content to standardize on the basis of the least advanced countries.[1] This Convention—and there are other examples—shows precisely the opposite tendency. On each of the separate provisions of the Convention particular countries can point to a more advanced condition in their own practice. But in no single country does the existing provision cover the whole requirements of the Convention. The Conference has accepted on every point the maximum that appeared to be reasonably practicable, and by embodying these in a single enactment has prescribed a standard that is, on the whole, more comprehensive and exacting than any that exists at present. No doubt this forward reaching spirit has its own dangers, unless it is restrained by constant reference to economic and administrative actualities. But, at least, it absolves the Conference from any charge of sloth and timorousness. And —what matters much more—it is typical of the temper and of the results of the association of nations in an enterprise of humane and sympathetic emulation. The direct, co-operative discussion of these problems is the longest step towards their solution. The ground thus gained can be less easily lost when so many interests from so many peoples are pledged to its defence.

[1] (See p. 19.)

Chapter IX

THE EMPLOYMENT OF CHILDREN

BESIDES the general question of the protection of women and children in unhealthy and dangerous processes, two distinct problems were raised in connexion with the employment of children. The first was that of the age at which children should be admitted to industrial employment, the second was the restriction of the employment of children during the night. Both these matters were the subjects of reports to the Conference by a Commission, which was drawn almost equally from the representatives of European and non-European countries.[1]

On the second problem, the recommendations of the Commission and the subsequent action of the Conference followed very closely the decisions which were taken in relation to women's work. The Berne Conference of 1913 had drafted a Convention prohibiting the employment during the night of young persons under sixteen years of age; and though the war intervened to prevent the full realization of the Berne programme, several States had already adopted this limitation. A few States, including Great Britain, France, and Denmark, had indeed prescribed eighteen as the minimum age.

(1) Employment of children during the night.

The Commission was unanimous in advising the Conference to accept the higher age. The one case in which it seemed necessary to retain the lower limit was that of continuous shift industries where boys and men work together. Here it was agreed that boys over sixteen should be admitted to night work, in certain specified processes where their presence was known to be necessary. The term "night," conformably to the definition adopted in the regulation of the employment of women, was held to comprise a period of at least eleven consecutive hours, including the interval between 10 p.m. and 5 a.m. The difficulty of industries which worked two

[1] The Chairman was Sir Malcolm Delevingne (Great Britain).

shifts of eight hours in the seventeen hours between 5 a.m. and 10 p.m. naturally occurred in this Convention also. Curiously enough, in this case, although in relation to women's work it had been rejected by the Conference, M. Guérin's proposal to permit work from either 4 a.m. till 10 p.m., or from 5 a.m. till 11 p.m. (in either case shortening by one hour the period defined as " night "), was unanimously endorsed by the Commission. It was, however, again rejected by the full Conference, though narrowly (by thirty-eight votes to thirty-two), and apparently more or less as an afterthought, so that the two Conventions were brought into uniformity in this respect.

The application of the Convention thus drafted to the countries in which special industrial circumstances obtain gave rise to two distinct groups of cases—those of the devastated countries on the one hand, and the Oriental and tropical countries on the other. In the former case the Belgian employers' delegate urged that in some of the main industries of Belgium the Convention should not come into effect for a number of years. The Commission felt that the request was not unreasonable, though they were reluctant to sanction any long delay. It was therefore agreed to take no final decision on the point at the present Conference ; but, without inserting any special provision in the Convention, to reconsider at the Conference of 1921, in the light of the experience then available, its application to the devastated countries. In the second case, one general provision was agreed upon : that in tropical countries, where night work is often less exhausting than day work, the night period may be less than eleven hours if compensating rest is given in the middle of the day. On the question of the detailed modifications appropriate to the several Oriental countries, the main discussion centred naturally on Japan and on India. With regard to other Oriental countries, the information at the disposal of the Conference was too slight to enable any definite decision to be taken. Consideration was therefore deferred until the 1920 Conference. But recommendations were made—in this case without much difficulty—for the two chief countries of the East. For Japan it was agreed that until 1925 night employment should be prohibited to young persons under fifteen years of age ; thereafter the minimum age should be raised to sixteen. The Japanese legislature had recently fixed the mimimum age for night employment at fifteen ; but since the law was not to become operative for twelve years, the decision of the Conference (which was supported by the Japanese Government and employers' delegates), marks a substantial advance. In India, the age was fixed at fourteen for boys and eighteen for girls. The Convention applies only to factories as defined in the national law ; but the Conference in this connexion made the same urgent recommendation to the Government of India as it had made on the subject of hours of work— that the factory law should be amended so as to bring within its provisions establishments employing twenty persons.

Considerably greater difficulty was experienced both in the Commission and in the Conference in reaching decisions on the prior question of the general age of the admission of children into industrial employment. It was manifest throughout the discussions that the Conference was anxious to fix the minimum age as high as was seriously practicable. But in this case there was a special difficulty which did not arise in connexion with night work. In many countries, the age at which compulsory education ends is twelve. If children are not to be admitted to industry until they have reached the age of fourteen or fifteen, then under existing conditions they may be left for two or three years entirely without regular supervision or occupation, the results of which are certain to be disastrous. No useful legislation is possible on this subject unless it is clearly understood that the inevitable corollary to any raising of the age is the corresponding extension of the public responsibility for education. The Commission and the Conference were fully aware of this difficulty ; and in fixing the age of admission at fourteen they legislated up to the limit of what appeared to be, on the evidence available, the greatest possible extension of the educational systems of the States concerned. Some members of the Commission desired to fix the age at fifteen, or even sixteen, and have placed on record their view that the age of fourteen is acceptable only as a transitory and provisional measure. Others, again, though not disposed to question the wisdom of legislating for an age of fourteen, felt that to bring the Convention into effect in July, 1922, left too little time for the necessary overhauling and extension of the educational machinery. The Conference, however, believed that it had fairly estimated

(2) *Minimum age of admission.*

the situation, and held to its decision. The matter is one
on which the clear balance of advantage lies in certainty
rather than in haste ; and the Conference did well to press for
no further advance than that which it seemed possible to
compass. It took the further precaution of drawing the
attention of the International Labour Office to the problem
of relating the educational and industrial ages, so that the
Office might consult with the Governments of the States
affected and propose the necessary measures.[1]

The remaining point of special interest in the Convention
was its application to Oriental countries. As in the preceding
case, nothing could be done at the moment in China, Persia,
and Siam ; and the Japanese Government
Japan. representatives were ready to submit proposals
which, with slight modification, received the
approval of the Commission and the Conference. It was
agreed that the provision of the present Japanese law, which
admits children under twelve to certain light and easy employments, should be repealed; that fourteen should be accepted
as the general minimum age, but that children over twelve
who had satisfactorily completed their courses in the elementary school might be admitted into industry. It will plainly
be the duty of the Conference at a later date to move for the
abolition of this exception, which might easily have undesir-
able educational results. But on the present occasion it
was very willing to accept the proposed arrangement, both
as in itself a considerable advance, and as a satisfactory
instalment of progress towards Japan's full acceptance of
the provisions of the Convention.

The case of India gave rise to greater difficulty. The law
at present permits the employment of children at the age
of nine ; and it seemed impossible both to
India. the Commission and to the Conference to set
any mark of approval on such a condition of
things. The representatives of the Government of India

---

[1] One point in connexion with this problem seems to have escaped
attention. The Convention applies only to industrial undertakings,
though it is proposed at some subsequent Conference to draft a similar
Convention for agriculture and commerce. If this course is long
delayed, then in any country in which there exists a gap between the
end of the period of compulsory education and the age fixed for entry
to industry there will be a drift into agricultural and commercial
employments, the latter of which, at least, has more " blind alleys "
than industry. The remedy, of course—fortunately within the power
of the Conference—is the early drafting of the second Convention.

told their now familiar tale that the Government was already considering the raising of the age, but was prevented from reaching an immediate decision by the inadequacy of Indian educational equipment. They therefore desired that no decision should be taken on the modifications appropriate to India until the Government had had an opportunity to conclude its deliberations and to bring its proposals before the Conference. This position was accepted by a majority of the Commission, though it was vigorously contested there, especially by the workers' delegates. The latter carried their protest to the Conference itself, and the main incident of the debate on the report of the Commission was the consideration of their amendment.

Miss Margaret Bondfield, on behalf of the British Labour delegation, moved that in India the age of admission should be fixed at twelve in factories using mechanical power, and employing not less than ten persons, in mines, in railways, and in docks. It was a moderate enough proposal, touching only the heavy and organised industries of India, and leaving out of account the great national employment in agriculture and domestic industry. Miss Bondfield's admirable fighting speech emphasized the responsibility of the Government of India for the alleged defectiveness of the educational apparatus ; and held that in the industrial development of India, conducted largely by British employers, the native workers were entitled to the same safeguards as those which had proved to be essential in Western industry. The most interesting parts of the debate were sustained by two Indian representatives : Mr. Chatterjee on behalf of the Government, and Mr. Joshi on behalf of the workers. The Government case could hardly have been better put than by one who so obviously sympathized with the desire to raise the status of the Indian worker, but who knew the difficulties, economic and psychological, in the way of any reformist movement. Mr. Joshi, on the other hand, admitting that the Government could not, in the time at its disposal, make very great changes in the educational system, yet thought that, given the stimulus, a great deal could be done to make effective the limitations proposed. He believed, moreover, that definitely to forbid the employment of children under twelve would remove one of the great obstacles to the universal introduction of compulsory education in India—the desire of white employers to obtain a supply of juvenile workers.

The workers' amendment carried by a substantial majority —thirty nine votes to twenty-one. Miss Bondfield, in proposing it, seems to have contemplated the likelihood of its rejection by the Government of India, and to have desired its adoption by the Conference mainly as an indication of its attitude to Indian Labour conditions. But it may well be that the Government will be compelled to regard as something more than a gesture a resolution which commanded the support, not only of Labour delegates of Great Britain and of the other participating countries, but of many Government representatives as well.

The whole Convention was adopted by ninety-one votes to three—the minority being the representatives of the Government and employers of India. The main provisions, therefore, were unanimously accepted. The Conference gave its whole weight to the enactment of a standard, which is higher than that obtaining even in many advanced industrial countries, and whose universal adoption, if for no other reason than its educational implications; will necessarily produce profound industrial and social changes. It so happened that the Convention on the age of admission to industry was the first which the Conference adopted. It was a fortunate inauguration of the work of the International Labour Legislature that its first act should have been so wholehearted an effort to secure to the children of the world a prolongation of the days of their youth and of preparation for the duties and responsibilities of industry and of citizenship.

Chapter X

THE INTERNATIONAL LABOUR OFFICE

THE record of the enactments on the employment of children concludes this brief survey of the legislative activities of the first Conference. It accomplished a considerable volume of work, and initiated the exploration of many more problems than those on which it came to a decision. There is occupation enough for more than one subsequent Conference in the consideration of the matters which were referred back for further study and report. The final duty of the Conference was to decide which of the many suggestions that had been made should be placed on the agenda of the next Conference. But after some discussion it was resolved to leave the selection of the business wholly in the hands of the International Labour Office. In pursuance of an arrangement made at Paris, the Conference of 1920 (to be held in Genoa in June and July) will be mainly concerned with the application to seamen of the Conventions enacted at Washington. But no doubt the opportunity will be used to consider some further important matters.

Agenda of the next Conference.

There remains to be recorded one further act of the Conference, in some ways the most significant of all its doings. In Washington, the International Labour Office, the permanent executive body of the Organisation was officially inaugurated. The Charter of the Organisation prescribes the main lines of the structure and functions of the Office. The Office is to be established at the seat of the League of Nations, as part of its fabric. The expenses of its management, together with the expenses incurred in the administration of Conferences, are to be met from the general funds of the League ; [1] and the Secretary-General of the League has the right to audit the accounts of the Office. The general control of the Office is vested in a

The Office.

Structure.

[1] See Art. 13, p. 118.

Governing Body of twenty-four members, which is constituted of the same elements and in the same proportions as the Conference. Twelve members are representatives of Governments, six of employers, and six of workpeople. Eight of the Government representatives are nominated directly by the Governments of the eight Powers " of chief industrial importance." The remaining four are nominated by those Governments which are selected for this purpose by a meeting of the Government delegates at the Conference, excluding the delegates of the eight States which already have the right of nomination.[1]

The representatives of the employers and workers are chosen, without any restriction of membership, by the Delegates of these constituencies to the Conference. The members of the Governing Body hold office for three years. It is left to that Body itself, subject to the approval of the Conference, to determine the method of filling vacancies.

The Governing Body appoints a Chairman from among its members, regulates its own procedure, and fixes its times of meeting. It has also to appoint a permanent head of the Office, in the person of the Director, who will assume responsibility for the conduct of the Office, and carry out, through his Office, the duties assigned to him by the Governing Body. All subordinate appointments are entrusted to the Director. The Charter stipulates only that a Deputy-Director should be elected, that with due regard to the efficiency of the Office the staff should be drawn from different nationalities, and that a certain number of its members should be women. Within those limitations the Director has complete freedom in the choice of his assistants.

The functions of the Office are, in the first instance, to collect

[1] It appears originally to have been proposed by the Labour Commission at Paris that, for purposes of the election of Government representatives to the Governing Body, the parallel of the Assembly and the present Executive Council of the League should be followed. While, as regards representation at the Conference, all States and their self-governing Dominions were to be regarded as separate units; for the purposes of this election they were to be regarded as together constituting one unit. The effect, of course, would have been to confer full rights of membership of the Conference on all the British Dominions (including India), but to appoint to the Governing Body only one Government representative of the whole Empire. This course, however, was not adopted by the Peace Conference. For all purposes in the Labour Organisation the Mother Country and the Dominions are regarded as distinct units.

and distribute information " on all subjects relating to the international adjustment of conditions of industrial life." To
this end it is charged to issue a periodical journal
Functions.   in English and French and such other languages as may be thought desirable, dealing with problems of industry and employment of international interest. It will also carry out such special investigations as the Conference may desire, and perform such administrative and other duties as the Conference may assign to it. How important these may become is clear from the record of the first Conference. The Washington Conference called for further study of several complex questions relating to health, unemployment, and the difficulties arising in different forms of the regulation of industrial conditions. And in the course of a single Convention, the Office was directed not only to assemble in the most convenient form the data supplied by the different Governments for the comparative study of Unemployment, but also to assume the arduous administrative duty of co-ordinating the operations of the various national systems of employment exchanges.

Above all, it falls to the Office to undertake the preparatory and consequent work for the annual Conferences. Sound legislation, and therefore the prestige of the whole Organisation, depends on the success with which the Office accomplishes this task. It must acquire and assimilate all the information and experience bearing on the proposed work of the Conference. It must think out the implications of every suggestion, and foresee, as far as human knowledge can, the difficulties and the advantages of every alternative method of approaching a particular problem ; and it must present the result of its researches in a form that will make them effectively serviceable in the deliberations of the Conference. Its fundamental business is to see that the Conference is in every way equipped for its work, and that it has no opportunity either to fail in some necessary duty or to exceed a wise interpretation of its commission.

It is therefore hardly too much to believe that upon the Office, more than upon any other single factor within the control of the Organisation, depends the future of international labour legislation. Whether or not it will be adequate to this exacting service is for the future to declare. It has not yet been subjected to the test of actual experience, even in the measure in which the Conference has been tried :

for the three months that have passed since its inauguration at Washington have been barely sufficient to determine lines of organisation, to gather the nucleus of a staff, and to fulfil the duties consequent upon the closing of the first Conference. All that can be said is that it has started its career under vigorous direction, and at a moment when its work, though perhaps more difficult than in normal times, has yet the opportunity to win for itself a wide and loyal recognition.

At Washington, the first Governing Body of the Office was elected. An initial difficulty was experienced owing to the failure of the Council of the League [1] to adjudicate between competing claims from different countries to rank among the eight States of " chief industrial importance," which had the right of direct nomination. The Organising Committee, with a view to facilitating the decision, had drawn up a provisional list of the States which might be regarded as belonging to this category. Objection, however, was taken to this list by five States, which were not included in it : Canada, Poland, Sweden, Spain, and India. No decision was rendered on the protest before the end of the Washington Conference, and the Conference was compelled, in view of the urgency of the establishment of the Office, to act without waiting for a settlement of the question. The right to nominate directly was therefore accorded to the eight States named by the Organising Committee, the United States, Great Britain, France, Germany, Italy, Belgium, Japan, and Switzerland. The Government delegates of the other participating States met in order to select the Governments which should nominate to the four remaining seats. The choice fell upon Spain, Argentina, Canada, and Poland. The fifth State, in order of preference, was Denmark ; and since, owing to the delay in the ratification of the Treaty by the United States, that country was not at the moment eligible for membership, Denmark was invited to exercise the right of nomination until the United States entered the League.

The employers' and workers' delegates met in separate sessions in order to appoint their members. The employers chose representatives from Great Britain, France, Italy, Belgium, Czecho-Slovakia, and the United States ; but pending the appointment of the last named a representative of Switzerland. The workers nominated representatives from

[1] The Council had not then been constituted.

France, Holland, Great Britain, Sweden, and, until the entry of the United States, from Canada. The sixth place they reserved for a representative of the German workers.[1]

The three sets of elections proceeded independently, and the results, when they were set together, gave a curiously one-sided body. On the present Governing Body, Great Britain and France each have three representatives ; Italy, Belgium, Germany, Switzerland, and Canada have two. With the entry of the three representatives of the United States the area of membership will be narrowed still further. Of the twenty-four members, twenty are drawn from European countries. There is one representative of South America, and one of Japan. South Africa, India, China, and other parts of the world which are likely to be affected by the activities of the Organisation have no part in membership at all.

Protests, naturally, were immediately forthcoming. When the results of the elections were announced, two South American delegates intimated their dissent from an arrangement which assigned to the twenty Latin-American States-members of the Organisation one seat out of twenty-four, and their objection was energetically supported by the South African delegates. On the closing day of the Conference the latter delegation formally proposed a resolution expressing the disapproval of the Conference at the predominance of European representatives on the Governing Body. On a record vote, the motion carried by forty-four to thirty-nine—the minority containing only one non-European vote, the majority containing not only the extra-European delegations but the representatives of Great Britain and Spain.

The existing situation is clearly unsatisfactory. It is true that Europe must necessarily preponderate on the Governing Body—partly because of the concentration of industrial interests in Europe, and partly because the European representatives alone have easy access to the two-monthly sessions of the Governing Body at Geneva. But the present degree of preponderance is indefensible ; and before the end of the Washington Conference the Governing Body had given an indication of its intention to revise its own composition.[2]

[1] A list of the members of the Governing Body will be found in Appendix IV, p. 190.

[2] M. Fontaine, Chairman of the Body, proposed that the question should be put on the agenda of the next Conference.

On the other hand, it is equally evident that the position is not the outcome of any attempt on the part of European delegates to secure a favourable position for themselves. The root of the difficulty is the mode of election prescribed by the Treaty. The method has much to commend it, and it was clearly designed to give to every constituency in the Conference the opportunity to elect its representatives with complete freedom. But each group acts in ignorance of what the others are doing, so that, within each group, the choice naturally tends to fall upon the representatives of the States which have had the greatest industrial experience. The result inevitably is a convergence upon the great manufacturing countries of Europe, and their undue predominance in the Governing Body as a whole.

It will be a delicate, but not impossible, undertaking to arrange some method of consultation between the groups which, without interfering with their essential autonomy in the choice of their representatives, will yet secure a more equitable distribution of membership. Something of the kind must clearly be done if the Governing Body is to possess, in a way in which it does not now possess, the confidence of the Conference and of the Members of the Organisation. But when this preliminary difficulty is overcome the Body thus elected promises to be one well equipped in status and in experience for the important duties which it has to fulfil in the new international order.

The newly constituted Body held two sessions in Washington. At its first meeting it conferred upon M. Arthur Fontaine, the representative of the French Government, the honour of becoming its first permanent Chairman. Of the appropriateness of this choice no two opinions could be entertained. M. Fontaine's work for the cause of international labour legislation in the years before the War, his Secretaryship of the Labour Commission at the Peace Conference, his Chairmanship of the Organising Committee and of the Commission on Selection, and the part which he had played in the Conference itself, had marked him out as in every way worthy of the honour. The directorship of the Office was provisionally entrusted to M. Albert Thomas, who had given conspicuous service to the Trade Union, Labour and co-operative movements of France, and who during the War was Minister of Munitions. The election of M. Thomas was formally con-

Appoint-ments.

firmed by the first full meeting of the Governing Body held in Europe, and he has now entered upon the duties of his office.   The Director has before him a most arduous and responsible task, for, in a more immediate and personal way than any other, he must shape the future of this critical experiment in internationalism.   It is fortunate for the Office and for the Organisation that it has found a man of such experience, resourceful energy, and constructive power.

M. Thomas has already made his most important subordinate appointment.   His choice of Mr. H. B. Butler as Deputy-Director appeared inevitable to those who took part in the Washington Conference, and they will applaud its wisdom.   The Office is no more than in process of building. The main lines of its organisation appear to be easily laid down. A diplomatic division will deal with the preliminary and consequent business of the Conferences, and will conduct all the negotiations with Governments, especially in connexion with the administration of the enactments of the Conference; a scientific division will be responsible for the general research and publication work of the Office; while there will also be a number of special technical branches, which will assist the two main divisions with all available information bearing on certain large provinces of industrial life.   Thus Emigration and Unemployment, Seamen, Agriculture, Social Insurance, and Hygiene are already alloted to such branches, and further studies will no doubt be undertaken.

At the moment the greater part of the strength of the office is absorbed in carrying through the procedure necessary to give effect to the Washington Conventions, and in preparing for the June Conference at Genoa.   But it has also begun, in a tentative way, the publication of its journal, initiated the special investigations called for at Washington, and has proposed to the League an inquiry into the working of the new political and economic organisation in Russia. Its tasks will grow from day to day with its resources.   One is fain to hope for a speedy rising of the tide of both.

Chapter XI

CONCLUSIONS

IN the course of this rapid survey attention has already been drawn to some points of special significance for the future of the Labour Organisation. But it may be convenient to bring them together in this concluding chapter, and to offer some observations on the working of the Organisation so far as it has already gone.

No one, perhaps, would be disposed seriously to question the success of the Washington Conference. It worked under

The spirit of the Conference. difficult mechanical and psychological conditions; it had to explore the whole technique of its procedure, and learn to accommodate itself to the many exigencies of a polyglot assembly.

In some respects it was more fortunate than later Conferences are likely to be, but probably no future Conference will have to spend so long a time in learning the conditions and the routine of its work. Nevertheless, it set its seal upon many important agreements, and gave to these a degree of unanimous support which, at the outset, could never have been forecast. And, in the main, the Conventions and Recommendations which it passed were far from being pious generalities which imposed no very definite obligations on those who accepted them. They were, as far as the nature of the case allowed, precise, detailed, and explicit, and left no ambiguity as to what they were intended to achieve. This the Conference was able to do, because with, on the whole, astonishingly little pedantry, and with a sense of its obligation to reach concrete and articulate enactments on the subjects before it, it laboured with good humour, patience, and industry, and in a spirit of conciliation, touched now and then with a certain exaltation of purpose.

The next step in the history of the Organisation does not lie in its own power. It rests with the Governments who sent their representatives to participate in its work.

Attitude of Governments. If, possibly even at the cost of some small sacrifice, they are ready to ratify the Conventions and to accept the Recommendations enacted at Washington, the prestige and the responsibility of the Conference—and with it of the League of Nations—will at once be greatly enhanced. If, on the other hand, they are slow to conform to the findings of the Conference, then the task of the Organisation becomes, not indeed impossible, but more difficult and to some degree more hazardous. Like most other institutions it is apt to be wise and effective in proportion to the weight of responsibility which it carries. If in future its acts are found to possess no real moral authority, the cohesion and practical quality of the Conference will be much harder to maintain. The indifference of Governments is bound to affect the spirit of the Conference itself.

There is therefore a certain gravity and momentousness attaching to the decisions which all national Governments must shortly take on the Washington Conventions. To treat them lightly would be to weaken not only the Labour Organisation, but the whole international enterprise. There is nothing in the Charter which requires Governments to adhere. But the whole motive of the Organisation lies in the hope that it affords of responsible co-operative legislation. If Governments, acting strictly within their legal rights, decline to conform to a Convention simply because it does not come in every detail within the four corners of their projected domestic policy, they retard the development of that international movement to which they had given their support.

It ought to be said here that a very special measure of responsibility rests upon the British Government. If one looks through the list of the Chairman of the Commissions in which the Conference did the great bulk of its legislative work one realizes the part which the British delegation took in shaping Conference policy. Other delegations may conceivably occupy more space in the record of the Conference proceedings ; but no delegation exercised an influence at all comparable to that of Great Britain. Moreover, in the world situation, as it is to-day, and especially with the temporary withdrawal of the United States from the League, there is no sort of doubt that the immediate future of international institutions depends primarily on the loyalty of Great Britain and the British Dominions. The adherence of Great Britain to the decisions of an international assembly, in the foundation and conduct of which it took a leading share, would be a powerful buttress to the whole international system. Its failure to adhere could have no other effect than to perpetuate among those of other nations who care for international ideals the false tradition of British cynicism and hypocrisy.

This matter of the attitude of Governments to the findings of the Conference brings into view two questions of the status of delegates which are of great importance to the success of the Organisation.

The first, and less fundamental, is the shortness of each delegate's term of office. A certain continuity is provided for in the composition of the Governing Body. *Continuity of representation.* Elections to that office are made for a period of three years. Even here it would be an advantage, which might easily be compassed, to arrange for the annual election of one-third of the Body, so that a greater measure of continuity would be maintained from year to year than by the present system of the election of the whole Body at triennial intervals. But, as regards the Conference, elections may be made by Governments, employers, and workers alike, solely for the duration of a single meeting. There is, indeed, no constitutional provision thus limiting the term of membership. But it is clearly intended that nominations are to be made for each Conference separately ; and the duration of any delegate's membership is entirely in the hands of his appointing Body. It is hard to see what other arrangement is possible. The foundation of the authority of the Conference is the freedom which all constituent organisations enjoy in the appointment of their delegates ; and it is not worth while obscuring or limiting that freedom in any way in the interests of continuity of membership. At the same time the Conference will suffer if too catastrophic changes in its composition should occur. Its effectiveness depends considerably on the ease with which the members settle down to their work and acquire some acquaintance with procedure, personalities, and forces. Without substantial continuity each Conference will have to learn its work afresh ; and, since most delegates are men in whose charge lie important interests at home, so that the Conference must confine its deliberations within definite limits of time, there may recur, towards the close of each meeting, the harassing pressure of business which was experienced at Washington.

The only possible safeguard is one which the success of the

Conference will itself create. When it is understood what membership of the Conference implies, and what weight may attach to its decisions, appointing bodies will tend to be careful in the selection of their representatives, and in their own interest, as well as in that of the Conference, to be slow to effect unnecessary change. It is a point of no small importance to all the constituent elements of the Conference that at an international assembly their view should be upheld by the best men available. It is probable enough that when any organisation has found a competent representative, who is willing to undertake the very considerable labour of participating in a Conference, it will be reluctant to release him.

A more difficult point emerges in connexion with the degree of authority which ought to be entrusted by their nominating bodies to the members of the Conference. *Delegate or Representative?* To some extent the question affects all such bodies ; but, in view of the special obligations devolving upon Governments, it affects the Governments somewhat critically. The Treaty uniformly refers to members as delegates ; the business of the Conference plainly requires that they should enjoy the powers of representatives. It is imperative, of course, that members should have ample opportunity for consultation with their authorities on the subjects to be considered at the Conference. They must be informed as to the general policy which their authorities would be prepared to support. Without this their counsel and their votes would both alike be deprived of much of their value. But it is clear that within these general instructions it is desirable to leave room for negotiation. The Conference, in principle, is a treaty-making body. On many occasions at Washington this aspect of its activity was manifest. Especially in relation to Oriental countries, where there appeared to be, even more than among European countries, a fear of the effects of competition, adjustments were continually on foot between different States. One country would agree to apply a particular clause to its own industry if another would accept a corresponding limitation. And in all the Commissions of the Conference pressure was continually brought to bear on the representatives of this country or of that, to accept some provision which would clear the way for the action of another country. Japan, India, China, South Africa were all in turn subject to this kind of influence. In the same way, not so much as between countries as between interests, the European members worked out mutual adjustments. The labour group was prepared to concede one point if the employers would concede another. Even the Government representatives were not exempt from pressure by a combination of the other interests.

All this interplay of forces is relevant in the highest degree to the purpose of the Conference. It is, indeed, the only way in which it can ever reach results. Its main business is just to facilitate by this very process of comparison and mutual adjustment the adoption of higher standards in each country than might otherwise be easily attainable. But plainly it is possible only within very narrow limits, if every member is bound too rigidly by his instructions. It is therefore desirable, even essential, that all appointing authorities, and especially Governments, should regard their nominees not only as delegates, but as representatives, or, in a sense, plenipotentiaries, who have the right and the duty, subject to a wide general control, to enter into detailed engagements, which these authorities, except for the gravest reasons, are prepared to accept.

It might be held that there is one advantage to the Conference in having the status of its members defined as that of delegates. A Government, for example, may regard itself as bound more definitely by the vote of its delegate than by a vote of its representative. If there were much substance in this contention it would be well for the Conference to accept the restriction of the range of its possible achievement that would follow from a recognition of the delegate status of its members. But, in fact, a Government which is sufficiently in earnest about internationalism to face the issue of delegation and representation, and deliberately to confer the wider powers on its nominees, is certain to feel itself as deeply implicated in the votes of one sort as in the votes of the other. The willingness of any Government to accept a Convention will depend in most cases, not so much on the policy at the Conference of its own representatives—though that is clearly an important and valid consideration—hardly at all on the precise status of those who express its view, but fundamentally on the degree of its loyalty to the ideal of international cooperation.

Here again, perhaps, important though the point is, no definite constitutional solution is possible. *Solvitur ambu-*

lando. There was at Washington a considerable diversity of practice among the Government members in this respect. Some delegations—as, for example, the Japanese—plainly took the view that they had authority to vary the exact letter of their instructions. Others, such as that of India, felt themselves bound to refuse, except in the most minute particulars, any concession in advance of what their Governments had prescribed, with the result that the only instance in which an enactment specially affecting a particular country was passed against the direct vote of the Government representatives of that country, was the clause relating to India in the Convention on the age of admission of children to industry. The status of delegate is not favourable for the discharge of the duties which the work of the Conference imposes on its members. But it will be changed, and Governments will accept responsibility for the votes of the nominees to whom they have assigned the larger function, in so far as the Conference succeeds in winning for itself the confidence of the more hopeful and progressive forces in its constituent countries.

It is worth while, perhaps, to say here that the same kind of responsibility devolves, not only upon Governments, but upon other nominating bodies. The Governments are legally entrusted with the duties, first of ratifying or rejecting, and secondly of administering, the Conventions. But the seriousness with which they will accept these obligations depends to some degree on the concern which their partners in the Conference show for the effectiveness of its work. If the Employers' Associations or the Trade Unions are either indifferent or hostile, it is less easy for a well-intentioned Government to be in earnest with its international duties, and more easy for one which is disposed to take them lightly so to regard them. Especially is this true of the administration of the Conventions. The whole machinery of the sanctions of the Organisation has been so constructed that the only effective force behind it is publicity. Publicity depends on the vigilance of the interests affected ; and it is their business, if they make any profession of faith in internationalism, not only to make much of their selection of a delegate, and to inform him of their view, but to be willing to be instructed by him, and after a decision has been taken to support him with the strength of their organisation.

Apart from these more or less external conditions, and as

a means to the satisfactory attainment of them, two things seem to be imperative for the success of the Conference. The first, which it is mainly the duty of the Office to supply, is full and exact information as to the implications of any suggested legislation. Legislation without such preparatory work, especially on problems so complex as those which the Conference will be called upon to consider, is certain to be futile. The second—the corollary of this and of what has gone before—is that the Conference should abide resolutely by its brief. There must always be a subtle temptation to the Conference to extend the range of its enactments. The danger is not that some one may, of set purpose, try to induce the Conference to legislate on some unprepared topic or to force through some unexamined policy. The ordinary rules of constitution and procedure are a sufficient safeguard against that. It is that the Conference may trespass the limits, perhaps not very clearly defined, of the problem which it is considering, and append to its decision on that problem a further decision in some allied matter which was not explicitly before it. Its problems are many-sided ; and in the discussion of any one of them there may emerge some aspect or possible further application of its solution which is relevant and natural, but which is not within the terms of its immediate reference. It is easy enough, but fatally prejudicial, for the Conference, under the influence of some more ardent spirit, to give some positive judgment on such a point.

The desiderata of the Conference.

In this respect the Washington Conference was not wholly beyond reproach. On two points at least it may fairly be said to have exceeded a strict reading of its mandate. It passed a Recommendation on the subject of Reciprocity in the treatment of foreign workers, and it extended the Convention on the employment of women after childbirth to commerce as well as to industry. Both of these proposals were highly relevant to the questions before the Conference, and the references to the Conference were wide enough formally to cover both points. Both of them, very likely, are sound decisions. Nevertheless, the preliminary researches of the Organising Committee had not dealt seriously with either matter ; and no Government or other appointing body had had any opportunity of formulating a policy on them This latter is the crucial consideration. The Conference has still its authority to gain. It can gain it from no other source than from the confidence which the different national Governments can be induced to accord to it, and from the sincerity with which they observe their obligations towards it. It is a counsel of prudence, therefore, as well as of honour that the Conference should observe, with the same strictness as it expects from them, its obligations towards Governments and other nominating authorities. In statute and in intention the opportunity to consider beforehand all the Conference agenda is secured to these authorities ; and it is important that no invasion of that right should occur. The Conference has ample power of initiation. It can move to consider any subject which it chooses, but it must consent to a short delay in order, not only that it may be furnished with all the relevant material, but that the interests concerned may be consulted.

In all probability, from this point of view, the procedure of the Conference is capable of improvement. Something in the nature of a third reading debate on a Convention as a whole before it is put to a final vote might be an advantage. In principle, indeed, the opportunity for this is now provided under the rule which allows the president of the Conference, in consultation with the vice-presidents, to receive amendments to the final text of a Convention ; and no doubt the matter will receive further consideration in the light of the experience of the Conference.

There are a good many other difficulties to which the Conference is liable. It is not, and so long as it is vital can never be, an easy assembly to hold together. It is crossed and recrossed by important lines of divisions of interest, between different nationalities and temperaments, between Europe and the non-European world, between countries well endowed with workers and those which are in need of them, and, not least, between the different sections of every delegation. But with adequate preparation, and an understanding of the complexity of the issues with which the Conference deals, these differences are not likely to prove intractable. The progressive improvement of conditions in all countries, even the attainment of *substantial* equality, does not mean uniformity either in legislative or administrative provisions ; and the Conference will mistake the line of advance if it pursue the ideal of identity. Impatience, perhaps, is the most serious enemy with which it will have to contend in its own house.

It quite certainly can do little yet to alter profoundly the economic and industrial fabric of the world. That will be achieved only through the growth in every part of our civilization of a more humane philosophy of life, and a more conscientious and persistent endeavour to shape the material environment of human beings and their relations with one another in accordance with the moral necessities which rule the destiny of man. To that high end, perhaps, no organisation can be other than auxiliary ; none certainly, in its own right, is the sole or supreme instrument. But, at the least, the Labour Organisation, touching as it does the affairs of men on issues which, if they are not fundamental, are yet absorbing and carry the seeds of conflict, can effect many things in the way of a " removal of hindrances." It is no small task, and it is one which, if it prosper, must lead to a greater end. Whatever success is achieved here brings us nearer to a more stably poised and yet more finely responsive civilization, not merely and not chiefly by way of the betterment of our mechanism for external adjustment, but by opening to the organised good-will of men a new field for expression and for service. The power of an ideal to draw to itself the regard and devotion of men is immeasurably enhanced when it is " made flesh and dwells among us." Therein, far more than in any specific act, lies the significance of the League and of the Labour Organisation. By their faithfulness and wisdom in the discharge of those limited tasks which are assigned to them they may accomplish this good or that for the world. But their greatest honour will be thereby to kindle and to conserve the faith of men in potency of mutual service for the healing of the nations. Light and perilous as is their footing in the world of actuality, the dominant fact is that they *are* and that in their own way and in their own degree they may become centres of that quickening devotion to the good life in individuals and in communities which is alone the path hazardous in incident it may be, but certain in ultimate leading, to our abiding city.

APPENDIX I

[Part XIII of the Treaty was drafted by the Commission on International Labour Legislation. The Commission contained fifteen members, two representatives of each of the Great Powers—the United States, the British Empire, France, Italy, Japan, and Belgium; and one representative each from Cuba, Poland, and Czecho-Slovakia. Mr. Samuel Gompers was Chairman of the Commission; M. Arthur Fontaine and Mr. H. B. Butler were the Secretaries.

Most of the work and nearly all the recommendations of the Commission were based on a draft scheme submitted by the British representatives. The British scheme had been carefully discussed with several Trade Union leaders, including Messrs. Arthur Henderson and J. H. Thomas.

Mr. G. N. Barnes submitted the Report of the Commission to the plenary session of the Peace Conference.]

THE LABOUR SECTIONS OF THE PEACE TREATY

SECTION I.—PERMANENT ORGANISATION

(The figures in brackets are the numbers of the Articles in the Peace Treaty.)

PREAMBLE

Whereas the League of Nations has for its object the establishment of universal peace, and such a peace can be established only if it is based upon social justice;

And whereas conditions of labour exist involving such injustice, hardship and privation to large numbers of people as to produce unrest so great that the peace and harmony of the world are imperilled; and an improvement of those conditions is urgently required: as, for example, by the regulation of the hours of work, including the establishment of a maximum working day and week, the regulation of the labour supply, the prevention of unemployment, the provision of an adequate living wage, the protection of the worker against sickness, disease and injury arising out of his employment, the protection of children, young persons and women, provisions for old age and injury, protection of the interests of workers when employed in countries other than their own, recognition of the principle of freedom of association, the organisation of vocational and technical education and other measures ;

Whereas also the failure of any nation to adopt humane conditions of labour is an obstacle in the way of other nations which desire to improve the conditions in their own countries

The High Contracting Parties, moved by sentiments of justice and humanity, as well as by the desire to secure the permanent peace of the world, agree to the following :—

CHAPTER I

ORGANISATION

ARTICLE 1. (387.)

A permanent organisation is hereby established for the promotion of the objects set forth in the Preamble.

The original Members of the League of Nations shall be the original Members of this organisation, and hereafter membership of the League of Nations shall carry with it membership of the said organisation.

ARTICLE 2. (388.)

The permanent organisation shall consist of (i) a General Conference of Representatives of the Members and (ii) an International Labour Office controlled by the Governing Body described in Article 7.

ARTICLE 3. (389.)

The meetings of the General Conference of Representatives of the Members shall be held from time to time as occasion may require, and at least once in every year. It shall be composed of four Representatives of each of the Members of whom two shall be Government Delegates and the two other shall be Delegates representing respectively the employers and the workpeople of each of the Members.

Each Delegate may be accompanied by advisers, who shall not exceed two in number for each item on the agenda of the meeting. When questions specially affecting women are to be considered by the Conference, one at least of the advisers should be a woman.

The Members undertake to nominate non-Government Delegates and advisers chosen in agreement with the industrial organisations, if such organisations exist, which are most representative of employers or workpeople, as the case may be, in their respective countries.

Advisers shall not speak except on a request made by the Delegate whom they accompany and by the special authorisation of the President of the Conference, and may not vote.

A Delegate may by notice in writing addressed to the President appoint one of his advisers to act as his deputy, and the adviser, while so acting, shall be allowed to speak and vote.

The names of the Delegates and their advisers will be communicated to the International Labour Office by the Government of each of the Members.

The credentials of Delegates and their advisers shall be subject to scrutiny by the Conference, which may, by two-thirds of the votes cast by the Delegates present, refuse to admit any Delegate or adviser whom it deems not to have been nominated in accordance with this Article.

ARTICLE 4. (390.)

Every Delegate shall be entitled to vote individually on all matters which are taken into consideration by the Conference.

If one of the Members fails to nominate one of the non-Government Delegates whom it is entitled to nominate, the other non-Government Delegate shall be allowed to sit and speak at the Conference, but not to vote.

If in accordance with Article 3 the Conference refuses admission to a Delegate of one of the Members, the provisions of the present Article shall apply as if that Delegate had not been nominated.

ARTICLE 5. (391.)

The meetings of the Conference shall be held at the seat of the League of Nations, or at such other place as may be decided by the Conference at a previous meeting by two-thirds of the votes cast by the Delegates present.

ARTICLE 6. (392.)

The International Labour Office shall be established at the seat of the League of Nations as part of the organisation of the League.

ARTICLE 7 (393).

The International Labour Office shall be under the control of a Governing Body consisting of 24 persons, appointed in accordance with the following provisions :—

The Governing Body of the International Labour Office shall be constituted as follows :—

> Twelve persons representing the Governments,
> Six persons elected by the Delegates to the Conference representing the employers,
> Six persons elected by the Delegates to the Conference representing the workers.

Of the twelve persons representing the Governments eight shall be nominated by the Members which are of the chief industrial importance, and four shall be nominated by the Members selected for the purpose by the Government Delegates to the Conference, excluding the Delegates of the eight Members mentioned above.

Any question as to which are the Members of the chief industrial importance shall be decided by the Council of the League of Nations.

The period of office of the members of the Governing Body will be three years. The method of filling vacancies and other similar questions may be determined by the Governing Body subject to the approval of the Conference.

The Governing Body shall, from time to time, elect one of its members to act as its Chairman, shall regulate its own procedure and shall fix its own times of meeting. A special meeting shall be held if a written request to that effect is made by at least ten members of the Governing Body.

ARTICLE 8. (394.)

There shall be a Director of the International Labour Office, who shall be appointed by the Governing Body, and subject to the instructions of the Governing Body, shall be responsible for the efficient conduct of the International Labour Office and for such other duties as may be assigned to him.

The Director or his deputy shall attend all meetings of the Governing Body.

ARTICLE 9. (395.)

The staff of the International Labour Office shall be appointed by the Director, who shall, so far as is possible with due regard to the efficiency of the work of the Office, select persons of different nationalities. A certain number of these persons shall be women.

ARTICLE 10. (396.)

The functions of the International Labour Office shall include the collection and distribution of information on all subjects relating to the international adjustment of conditions of industrial life and labour, and particularly the examination of subjects which it is proposed to bring before the Conference with a view to the conclusion of international conventions, and the conduct of such special investigations as may be ordered by the Conference.

It will prepare the agenda for the meetings of the Conference.

It will carry out the duties required of it by the provisions of this part of the present Treaty in connection with international disputes.

It will edit and publish in French and English, and in such other languages as the Governing Body may think desirable, a periodical paper dealing with problems of industry and employment of international interest.

Generally, in addition to the functions set out in this article, it shall have such other powers and duties as may be assigned to it by the Conference.

ARTICLE 11. (397.)

The Government Departments of any of the Members which deal with questions of industry and employment may communicate directly with the Director through the Representative of their Government on the Governing Body of the International Labour Office, or failing any such Representative, through such other qualified official as the Government may nominate for the purpose.

ARTICLE 12. (398.)

The International Labour Office shall be entitled to the assistance of the Secretary-General of the League of Nations on any matter in which it can be given.

9

ARTICLE 13. (399.)

Each of the Members will pay the travelling and subsistence expenses of its Delegates and their advisers and of its Representatives attending the meetings of the Conference or Governing Body, as the case may be.

All the other expenses of the International Labour Office and of the meetings of the Conference or Governing Body shall be paid to the Director by the Secretary-General of the League of Nations out of the general funds of the League.

The Director shall be responsible to the Secretary-General of the League for the proper expenditure of all moneys paid to him in pursuance of this Article.

CHAPTER II

PROCEDURE

ARTICLE 14. (400.)

The agenda for all meetings of the Conference will be settled by the Governing Body, who shall consider any suggestion as to the agenda that may be made by the Government of any of the Members or by any representative organisation recognized for the purpose of Article 3.

ARTICLE 15. (401.)

The Director shall act as the Secretary of the Conference, and shall transmit the agenda so as to reach the Members four months before the meeting of the Conference, and, through them, the non-Government Delegates when appointed.

ARTICLE 16. (402.)

Any of the Governments of the Members may formally object to the inclusion of any item or items in the agenda. The grounds for such objection shall be set forth in a reasoned statement addressed to the Director, who shall circulate it to all the Members of the Permanent Organisation.

Items to which such objection has been made shall not, however, be excluded from the agenda if at the Conference a majority of two-thirds of the votes cast by the Delegates present is in favour of considering them.

If the Conference decides (otherwise than under the

preceding paragraph) by two-thirds of the votes cast by the Delegates present that any subject shall be considered by the Conference, that subject shall be included in the agenda for the following meeting.

ARTICLE 17. (403.)

The Conference shall regulate its own procedure, shall elect its own President, and may appoint committees to consider and report on any matter.

Except as otherwise expressly provided in this part of the present Treaty, all matters shall be decided by a simple majority of the votes cast by the Delegates present.

The voting is void unless the total number of votes cast is equal to half the number of the Delegates attending the Conference.

ARTICLE 18. (404.)

The Conference may add to any committees which it appoints technical experts, who shall be assessors without power to vote.

ARTICLE 19. (405.)

When the Conference has decided on the adoption of proposals with regard to an item in the agenda, it will rest with the Conference to determine whether these proposals should take the form : (a) of a recommendation to be submitted to the Members for consideration with a view to effect being given to it by national legislation or otherwise, or (b) of a draft international convention for ratification by the Members.

In either case a majority of two-thirds of the votes cast by the Delegates present shall be necessary on the final vote for the adoption of the recommendation or draft convention, as the case may be, by the Conference.

In framing any recommendation or draft convention of general application, the Conference shall have due regard to those countries in which climatic conditions, the imperfect development of industrial organisation, or other special circumstances make the industrial conditions substantially different, and shall suggest the modifications, if any, which it considers may be required to meet the case of such countries.

A copy of the recommendaton or draft convention shall be authenticated by the signature of the President of the Conference and of the Director, and shall be deposited with the Secretary-General of the League of Nations. The Secretary-General will communicate a certified copy of the recommendation or draft convention to each of the Members.

Each of the Members undertakes that it will, within the period of one year at most from the closing of the session of the Conference, or if it is impossible owing to exceptional circumstances to do so within the period of one year, then at the earliest practicable moment, and in no case later than eighteen months from the closing of the session of the Conference, bring the recommendation or draft convention before the authority or authorities within whose competence the matter lies for the enactment of legislation or other action.

In the case of a recommendation, the Members will inform the Secretary-General of the action taken.

In the case of a draft convention, the Member will, if it obtains the consent of the authority or authorities within whose competence the matter lies, communicate the formal ratification of the convention to the Secretary-General, and will take such action as may be necessary to make effective the provisions of such convention.

If on a recommendation no legislative or other action is taken to make a recommendation effective, or if the draft convention fails to obtain the consent of the authority or authorities within whose competence the matter lies, no further obligation shall rest upon the Member.

In the case of a federal State, the power of which to enter into conventions on labour matters is subject to limitations, it shall be in the discretion of that Government to treat a draft convention to which such limitations apply as a recommendation only, and the provisions of this article with respect to recommendations shall apply in such case.

The above article shall be interpreted in accordance with the following principle :—

In no case shall any Member be asked or required, as a result of the adoption of any recommendation or draft convention by the Conference, to lessen the protection afforded by its existing legislation to the workers concerned.

ARTICLE 20. (406.)

Any convention so ratified shall be registered by the Secretary-General of the League of Nations, but shall only be binding upon the Members which ratify it.

ARTICLE 21. (407.)

If any convention coming before the Conference for final consideration fails to secure the support of two-thirds of the votes cast by the Delegates present, it shall nevertheless be within the right of any of the Members of the Permanent Organisation to agree to such convention among themselves.

Any convention so agreed to shall be communicated by the Governments concerned to the Secretary-General of the League of Nations, who shall register it.

ARTICLE 22. (408.)

Each of the Members agrees to make an annual report to the International Labour Office on the measures which it has taken to give effect to the provisions of conventions to which it is a party. These reports shall be made in such form and shall contain such particulars as the Governing Body may request. The Director shall lay a summary of these reports before the next meeting of the Conference.

ARTICLE 23. (409.)

In the event of any representation being made to the International Labour Office by an industrial association of employers or of workers that any of the Members has failed to secure in any respect the effective observance within its jurisdiction of any convention to which it is a party, the Governing Body may communicate this representation to the Government against which it is made and may invite that Government to make such statement on the subject as it may think fit.

ARTICLE 24. (410.)

If no statement is received within a reasonable time from the Government in question, or if the statement when received is not deemed to be satisfactory by the Governing Body, the latter shall have the right to publish the representation and the statement, if any, made in reply to it.

ARTICLE 25. (411.)

Any of the Members shall have the right to file a complaint with the International Labour Office if it is not satisfied that any other Member is securing the effective observance of any convention which both have ratified in accordance with the foregoing articles.

The Governing Body may, if it thinks fit, before referring such a complaint to a Commission of Enquiry, as hereinafter provided for, communicate with the Government in question in the manner described in Article 23.

If the Governing Body does not think it necessary to communicate the complaint to the Government in question, or if, when they have made such communication, no statement in reply has been received within a reasonable time which the Governing Body considers to be satisfactory, the Governing Body may apply for the appointment of a Commission of Enquiry to consider the complaint and to report thereon.

The Governing Body may adopt the same procedure either of its own motion or on receipt of a complaint from a Delegate to the Conference.

When any matter arising out of Article 24 or 25 is being considered by the Governing Body, the Government in question shall, if not already represented thereon, be entitled to send a representative to take part in the proceedings of the Governing Body while the matter is under consideration. Adequate notice of the date on which the matter will be considered shall be given to the Government in question.

ARTICLE 26. (412.)

The Commission of Enquiry shall be constituted in accordance with the following provisions :—

Each of the Members agrees to nominate within six months of the date on which the present Treaty comes into force three persons of industrial experience, of whom one shall be a representative of employers, one a representative of workers, and one a person of independent standing, who shall together form a panel from which the members of the Commission of Enquiry shall be drawn.

The qualifications of the persons so nominated shall be subject to scrutiny by the Governing Body, which may by two-thirds of the votes cast by the representatives present refuse to accept the nomination of any person whose qualifications do not in its opinion comply with the requirements of the present article.

Upon the application of the Governing Body, the Secretary-General of the League of Nations shall nominate three persons, one from each section of this panel, to constitute the

Commission of Enquiry, and shall designate one of them as the President of the Commission. None of these three persons shall be a person nominated to the panel by any Member directly concerned in the complaint.

ARTICLE 27. (413.)

The Members agree that, in the event of the reference of a complaint to a Commission of Enquiry under Article 25, they will each, whether directly concerned in the complaint or not, place at the disposal of the Commission all the information in their possession which bears upon the subject-matter of the complaint.

ARTICLE 28. (414.)

When the Commission of Enquiry has fully considered the complaint, it shall prepare a report embodying its findings on all questions relevant to determining the issue between the parties and containing such recommendations as it may think proper as to the steps which should be taken to meet the complaint and the time within which they should be taken.

It shall also indicate in this report the measures, if any, of an economic character against a defaulting Government which it considers to be appropriate, and which it considers other Governments would be justified in adopting.

ARTICLE 29. (415.)

The Secretary-General of the League of Nations shall communicate the report of the Commission of Enquiry to each of the Governments concerned in the complaint, and shall cause it to be published.

Each of these Governments shall within one month inform the Secretary-General of the League of Nations whether or not it accepts the recommendations contained in the report of the Commission ; and if not, whether it proposes to refer the complaint to the Permanent Court of International Justice of the League of Nations.

ARTICLE 30. (416.)

In the event of any Member failing to take the action required by Article 19, with regard to a recommendation or draft Convention, any other Member shall be entitled to refer the matter to the Permanent Court of International Justice.

ARTICLE 31. (417.)

The decision of the Permanent Court of International Justice in regard to a complaint or matter which has been referred to it in pursuance of Article 29 or Article 30 shall be final.

ARTICLE 32. (418.)

The Permanent Court of International Justice may affirm, vary or reverse any of the findings or recommendations of the Commissions of Enquiry, if any, and shall in its decision indicate the measures, if any, of an economic character which it considers to be appropriate, and which other Governments would be justified in adopting against a defaulting Government.

ARTICLE 33. (419.)

In the event of any Member failing to carry out within the time specified the recommendations, if any, contained in the report of the Commission of Enquiry, or in the decision of the Permanent Court of International Justice, as the case may be, any other Member may take against that Member the measures of an economic character indicated in the report of the Commission or in the decision of the Court as appropriate to the case.

ARTICLE 34. (420.)

The defaulting Government may at any time inform the Governing Body that it has taken the steps necessary to comply with the recommendations of the Commission of Enquiry or with those in the decision of the Permanent Court of International Justice, as the case may be, and may request it to apply to the Secretary-General of the League to constitute a Commission of Enquiry to verify its contention. In this case the provisions of Articles 26, 27, 28, 29, 31 and 32 shall apply, and if the report of the Commission of Enquiry or the decision of the Permanent Court of International Justice is in favour of the defaulting Government, the other Governments shall forthwith discontinue the measures of an economic character that they have taken against the defaulting Government.

Chapter III

GENERAL

Article 35. (421.)

The Members engage to apply conventions which they have ratified in accordance with the provisions of this part of the present Treaty to their colonies, protectorates and possessions which are not fully self-governing :

1. Except where owing to the local conditions the convention is inapplicable, or
2. Subject to such modifications as may be necessary to adapt the convention to local conditions.

And each of the Members shall notify to the International Labour Office the action taken in respect of each of its colonies, protectorates and possessions which are not fully self-governing.

Article 36. (422.)

Amendments to this part of the present Treaty which are adopted by the Conference by a majority of two-thirds of the votes cast by the Delegates present shall take effect when ratified by the States whose representatives compose the Council of the League of Nations and by three-fourths of the Members.

Article 37. (423.)

Any question or dispute relating to the interpretation of this part of the present Treaty or of any subsequent Convention concluded by the Members in pursuance of the provisions of this part of the present Treaty shall be referred for decision to the Permanent Court of International Justice.

Chapter IV

TRANSITORY PROVISIONS

Article 38. (424.)

The first meeting of the Conference shall take place in October, 1919. The place and agenda for this meeting shall be as specified in the Annex hereto.

Arrangements for the convening and the organisation of the first meeting of the Conference will be made by the Government designated for the purpose in the said Annex. That Government shall be assisted in the preparation of the documents for submission to the Conference by an International Committee constituted as provided in the said Annex.

The expenses of the first meeting and of all subsequent meetings held before the League of Nations has been able to establish a general fund other than the expenses of Delegates and their advisers, will be borne by the Members in accordance with the apportionment of the expenses of the International Bureau of the Universal Postal Union.

ARTICLE 39. (425.)

Until the League of Nations has been constituted all communications which under the provisions of the foregoing articles should be addressed to the Secretary-General of the League will be preserved by the Director of the International Labour Office, who will transmit them to the Secretary-General of the League.

ARTICLE 40. (426.)

Pending the creation of a Permanent Court of International Justice, disputes which in accordance with this part of the present Treaty would be submitted to it for decision will be referred to a tribunal of three persons appointed by the Council of the League of Nations.

ANNEX

FIRST MEETING OF ANNUAL LABOUR CONFERENCE, 1919

The place of meeting will be Washington.

The Government of the United States of America is requested to convene the Conference.

The International Organising Committee will consist of seven members, appointed by the United States of America, Great Britain, France, Italy, Japan, Belgium and Switzerland. The Committee may, if it thinks necessary, invite other Members to appoint representatives.

Agenda—

1. Application of principle of the 8-hour day or of the 48-hour week.
2. Question of preventing or providing against unemployment.
3. Women's employment—
   (a) Before and after childbirth, including the question of maternity benefit.
   (b) During the night.
   (c) In unhealthy processes.
4. Employment of children.
   (a) Minimum age of employment.
   (b) During the night.
   (c) In unhealthy processes.
5. Extension and application of the International Conventions adopted at Berne in 1906 on the prohibition of night work for women employed in industry and the prohibition of the use of white phosphorus in the manufacture of matches.

SECTION II

GENERAL PRINCIPLES

ARTICLE 427.

The High Contracting Parties, recognizing that the well-being, physical, moral and intellectual, of industrial wage-earners is of supreme international importance, have framed in order to further this great end the permanent machinery provided for in Section I, and associated with that of the League of Nations.

They recognize that differences of climate, habits and customs, of economic opportunity and industrial tradition, make strict uniformity in the conditions of labour difficult of immediate attainment. But holding, as they do, that labour should not be regarded merely as an article of commerce, they think that there are methods and principles for regulating labour conditions which all industrial communities should endeavour to apply so far as their special circumstances will permit.

Among these methods and principles, the following seem to

the High Contracting Parties to be of special and urgent importance :—

>   *First.*—The guiding principle above enunciated that labour should not be regarded merely as a commodity or article of commerce.
>
>   *Second.*—The right of association for all lawful purposes by the employed as well as by the employers.
>
>   *Third.*—The payment to the employed of a wage adequate to maintain a reasonable standard of life as this is understood in their time and country.
>
>   *Fourth.*—The adoption of an eight hours day or a forty-eight hours week as the standard to be aimed at where it has not already been attained.
>
>   *Fifth.*—The adoption of a weekly rest of at least twenty-four hours, which should include Sunday wherever practicable.
>
>   *Sixth.*—The abolition of child labour and the imposition of such limitations on the labour of young persons as shall permit the continuation of their education and assure their proper physical development.
>
>   *Seventh.*—The principle that men and women should receive equal remuneration for work of equal value.
>
>   *Eighth.*—The standard set by law in each country with respect to the conditions of labour should have due regard to the equitable economic treatment of all workers lawfully resident therein.
>
>   *Ninth.*—Each State should make provision for a system of inspection in which women should take part, in order to ensure the enforcement of the laws and regulations for the protection of the employed.

Without claiming that these methods and principles are either complete or final, the High Contracting Parties are of opinion that they are well fitted to guide the policy of the League of Nations ; and that, if adopted by the industrial communities who are members of the League, and safeguarded in practice by an adequate system of such inspection, they will confer lasting benefits upon the wage-earners of the world.

APPENDIX II

LIST OF THE MEMBERS OF THE DELEGATIONS
TO THE
INTERNATIONAL LABOUR CONFERENCE
WASHINGTON, OCTOBER, 1919

OFFICERS

President, HON. W. B. WILSON (United States).
Vice-President, RIGHT HON. G. N. BARNES (Great Britain).
Vice-President, MR. JULES CARLIER (Belgium).
Vice-President, MR. LEON JOUHAUX (France).
Secretary-General, MR. H. B. BUTLER (Great Britain).
Legal Adviser, DR. MANLEY O. HUDSON (United States).

ARGENTINA

I.—*Government Delegates :*
> DR. LEONIDAS ANASTASI,
> DR. FELIPE ESPIL.

II.—*Employers' Delegate :*
> MR. HERMENEGILDO PINI.

III.—*Workers' Delegate :*
> MR. AMERICO BALINO.

> *Advisers :*
> MR. ALEJANDRO JOSEPH HAYES,
> DR. ALEJANDRO UNSAIN.

BELGIUM

I.—*Government Delegates :*
> MR. MICHEL LEVIE,
>> President of the Delegation, Minister of State,
>> Member of the Chamber of Representatives.

MR. ERNEST MAHAIM,
Professor at Liège University.

Advisers :
MR. ARMAND JULIN,
Permanent Secretary of the Labour Department.
MR. JOSEPH BRUGHMANS,
Chief Inspector of Factories.
MR. DESIRE GLIBERT,
General Inspector of the Labour Medical
Service.
MR. ALEXANDRE DELMER.
Principal Mining Engineer.

II.—*Employers' Delegate :*
MR. JULES CARLIER,
President of the Central Industrial Committee
for Belgium.

Advisers :
MR. LEON REPRIELS,
Chief of Section of the Ougrée Marihaye Steel
Works Co.
MR. MAURICE DE SMET DE NAYER,
Representative of the Textile Industries on the
Central Industrial Committee for Belgium.
MR. GEORGES DALLEMAGNE,
President of the Federation of Chemical
Industries for Belgium.
MR. ROCH BOULVIN,
Director-General of the Railway and Electric Co.
MR. MARCEL FRAIPONT,
Director-General of the Glass Works of Val
St.-Lambert.
MR. JULES LECOCQ,
Secretary and Treasurer of the Central Industrial
Committee for Belgium.

III.—*Workers' Delegate :*
MR. CORNEILLE MERTENS,
Secretary of the Trades Union Commission of
the Belgian Labour Party and of the Independent Trade Unions.

Advisers :
MR JOSEPH BAECK,
  Member of the Executive Council of the Trades
    Union Commission of the Labour Party and
    of the Independent Trade Unions, Provin-
    cial Secretary of the Metal Workers' Union.
MR. DUMONT,
  Federation of Liberal Workers, Antwerp.
MR. VICTOR PARY,
  Secretary of the General Confederation of
    Christian and Free Unions of Belgium.
MR. JOHN VAN DYCK,
  Treasurer of the General Confederation of
    Christian and Free Union of Belgium.
MR. GUILLAUME SOLAU,
  President of the Trades Union Commission of
    the Labour Party and of the Independent
    Trade Unions.
MR. EVARISTE VAN QUAQUEBEKE,
  General Secretary of the General Confederation
    of Christian and Free Unions of Belgium.
MISS HELENE BURNIAUX,
  Professor of St.-Gilles.
MISS VICTOIRE CAPPE,
  Vice-President of the General Confederation
    of Christian and Free Unions of Belgium.

BOLIVIA

Government Delegate :
DON IGNACIO CALDERON,
  Envoy Extraordinary and Minister Plenipoten-
    tiary of Bolivia at Washington.

BRAZIL

Government Delegates :
MR. AFANIO DE MELLO FRANCE,
MR. CARLOS CÆSAR DE OLIVEIRA SANPAIO.

CANADA

I.—*Government Delegates :*
  THE HON GIDEON D. ROBERTSON,
    Senator and Minister of Labour of Canada.

THE HON. NEWTON W. ROWELL, K.C., M.P.,
President of the Privy Council of Canada, and
Acting Secretary of State for External Affairs.

Advisers :

MR. F. A. ACLAND,
Deputy Minister of Labour of Canada.

MR. LORING C. CHRISTIE,
Legal Adviser to the Department of External
Affairs of Canada.

MR. DANIEL A. CAMERON, of Sydney,
Member of the Provincial Legislature of Nova
Scotia.

THE HON. C. W. ROBINSON, of Moncton,
Member without portfolio of the Government
of the Province of New Brunswick.

THE HON. W. L. MACKENZIE KING, C.M.G.,
M.P., of Ottawa,
Former Minister of Labour of Canada.

MR. LOUIS GUYON, of Montreal,
Deputy Minister of Labour for the Province of
Quebec.

DR. WALTER A. RIDDELL, of Toronto,
Deputy Minister of Labour for the Province
of Ontario.

THE HON. THOS. H. JOHNSON, of Winnipeg,
Attorney-General for the Province of Manitoba.

MR. T. M. MOLLOY, of Regina,
Secretary of the Bureau of Labour for the
Province of Saskatchewan.

THE HON. C. R. MITCHELL, of Edmonton,
Provincial Treasurer of the Province of Alberta.

MR. J. D. McNIVEN, of Victoria,
Deputy Minister of Labour for the Province
of British Columbia.

Secretary (and Adviser) :

MR. GERALD H. BROWN,
Secretary of the Reconstruction Committee of
the Government of Canada.

II.—*Employers' Delegate :*

MR. S. R. PARSONS,
President, British American Oil Company,
Limited, Royal Bank Building, Toronto.

Advisers :

MR. J. E. WALSH,
General Manager, Canadian Manufacturers' Association, Toronto.

MR. J. T. STIRRETT,
General Secretary, Canadian Manufacturers' Association, Toronto.

MR. E. BLAKE ROBERTSON,
Ottawa Representative, Canadian Manufacturers' Association, Ottawa.

MR. J. B. HUGG,
Canadian Manufacturers' Association, Winnipeg.

MR. J. G. MERRICK,
Secretary, Employers' Association, Toronto.

MR. JOHN R. SHAW,
Canada Furniture Manufacturers, Limited, Woodstock, Ontario.

MR. SAM HARRIS,
The Harris Lithographing Company, Ltd., Toronto.

III.—*Workers' Delegate :*

MR. P. M. DRAPER,
Secretary-Treasurer, Trades and Labour Congress of Canada, and President, Ottawa Typographical Union.

Advisers :

MR. TOM MOORE,
President, Trades and Labour Congress of Canada.

MR. ARTHUR MARTEL,
Vice-President, Trades and Labour Congress of Canada.

MR. ROBERT BAXTER,
Vice-President, Trades and Labour Congress of Canada.

MR. DAVID REES,
Vice-President, Trades and Labour Congress of Canada.

MRS. KATHLEEN DERRY,
Member, Boot and Shoe Workers' Union.

MR. ALEX McANDREW,
    Vice-President, Trades and Labour Congress
    of Canada, and Western Representative,
    United Brotherhood of Maintenance of Way
    Employees and Railway Shop Labourers.
MR. HARRY J. HALFORD,
    Vice-President, Trades and Labour Congress
    of Canada, Fifth Vice-President, Journeymen
    Barbers' International Union.

CHILI

Government Delegates:
MR. GUSTAVO MUNIZAGA VARELA,
MR. FELIX NIETO DEL RIO.

CHINA

Government Delegates:
MR. LINGOH WANG,
    Second Secretary of Legation.
MR. YUNG KWAI,
    Counsellor of Legation and Chargé d'Affaires
    ad interim.

Advisers:
MR. WU CHANG,
    Third Secretary of Legation.
MR. TSU-LI SUN,
    Attaché.
MR. PAN FRANCIS SHAH,
    Attaché.
MR. YUNG-CHING YANG,
    Chancellor of Legation.
MR. HSIAO WEI MIN,
    Chancellor of Legation.
MR. KENYON VANLEE DZUNG,
    Chancellor of Legation.

CZECHO-SLOVAKIA.

I.—*Government Delegates:*
MR. J. SOUSEK,
    Head of Department in Ministry of Social
    Welfare.
MR. CHARLES SPINKA,
    Inspector of Labour.

II.—*Employers' Delegates :*
>   MR. F. HODACZ,
>>   Secretary-General of Federation, Czecho-Slovak
>>   Manufacturers, Prague.

>   *Advisers :*
>>   MR. H. WALDES,
>>>   Manufacturer, Prague.
>>   MR. A. KRIZ,
>>>   Tailor, Prague.

III.—*Workers' Delegates :*
>   MR. R. TAYERLE, M.P.,
>>   Secretary, Czecho-Slovakian Federation of
>>   Labour, Prague.

>   *Advisers :*
>>   MR. F. STASTNY,
>>>   Secretary, Federation Metal Workers.
>>   MR. V. DUNDR,
>>>   Secretary, Czecho-Slovaque Federation of
>>>   Labour.
>>   MRS. M. STIVINOVA MAJEROVA,
>>>   Municipal Counsellor of Prague.
>>   MRS. LOUISA LANDOVA STYCHOVA,
>>>   Member of Parliament.

COLOMBIA

>   *Government Delegate :*
>>   DR. CARLOS ADOLFO URUETA,
>>>   Envoy Extraordinary and Minister Plenipoten-
>>>   tiary at Washington.

CUBA

I.—*Government Delegates :*
>   SR. CARLOS ARMENTEROS Y CARDENAS,
>>   Ex-Envoy Extraordinary, Ex-Minister to Vene-
>>   zuela, Assistant Secretary of Agriculture,
>>   Commerce and Labour.
>   SR. FRANSISCO CARRERA JUSTIZ,
>>   Ex-Minister to the United States, Spain and
>>   Mexico, and Professor of the University of
>>   Habana.

Advisers :

SENORA LAURA G. DE ZAYAS BAZAN,
   Professor in the Normal School of Havana.

SR. LUIS MARINO PEREZ,
   Librarian of the House of Representatives.

SR. CARLOS LOVEIRA.
   Ex-Delegate of the American Federation of
   Labour to South America.

Attaché :

DR. PABLO CARRERA JUSTIZ.

II.—*Employers' Delegates :*

SR. LUIS ROSAINZ Y DE LOS REYES,
   Ex-Magistrate.

DENMARK

I.—*Government Delegates :*

MR. S. NEUMANN,
   President of the Labour Council, Chief of Bureau
   of the Department of Labour and Social
   Insurance, Ministry of Interior.

MR. C. V. BRAMSNAES,
   Member of Parliament, Secretary in the
   Statistical Department.

Advisers :

MRS. MARIE HJELMER,
   Member of Parliament.

MR. BERTHEL DAHLGAARD,
   Deputy Chief of the Statistical Bureau of
   Copenhagen.

MR. SVEND TRIER,
   Deputy Chief Inspector of Factories and Workshops.

II.—*Employers' Delegate :*

MR. H. VESTESEN,
   Representative of the Central Federation of
   Labour Employers.

Advisers :

MR. H. C. OERSTED,
   Chief of Bureau of said Federation.

III.—*Workers' Delegate :*
> MR. C. F. MADSEN,
>> President of Amalgamated Federation of Labour Unions.

> *Adviser :*
> MR. P. HEDEBOL,
>> Member of Parliament, Member of the Copenhagen Town Council.

> *Secretary :*
> MR. R. LASSEN,
>> Deputy Chief of Bureau of the Department of Labour and Social Insurance.

> *Interpreter :*
> MR. H. H. SCHROEDER,
>> Secretary in Ministry of Interior.

ECUADOR

> *Government Delegates :*
> DR. DON RAFAEL H. ELIZALDE,
> DR. DON JUAN CUEVA GARCIA.

EL SALVADOR

> *Government Delegate :*
> DON SALVADOR SOL,
>> Envoy Extraordinary and Minister Plenipotentiary.

FINLAND

> I.—*Government Delegates :*
> MR. A. H. SAASTAMOINEN,
>> Envoy Extraordinary and Minister Plenipotentiary at Washington.
> JUDGE NIILO A MANNIO,
>> Secretary-General, Labour Dept. of Finland.

> II.—*Employers' Delegate :*
> MR. ROBERT LAVONIUS,
>> Mechanical Engineer, President Metal Employers' Federation of Finland.

III.—*Workers' Delegate:*

MR. MATTI PASSIVUERI,

President, Trade Union Organisation of Finland, Member of Parliament, formerly Social Minister.

FRANCE.

I.—*Government Delegates:*

MR. ARTHUR FONTAINE,

Director of the Labour Department, Ministry of Labour, Chairman of Executive Committee of the French State Railways.

MR. MAX LAZARD,

Secretary-General of the French Association for Combating Unemployment.

Advisers:

MR. P. BOULIN,

Divisional Labour Inspector.

MRS. LETELLIER,

Labour Inspectress.

MR. TONY REYMOND,

Assistant Director, Ministry of Public Works, General Secretary of the French State Railways.

II.—*Employers' Delegate:*

MR. LOUIS GUERIN,

Director of the Division of Linen Industry of France, Member of the Supreme Labour Council.

Advisers:

MR. COLLINET,

Professor in the Law Faculty of Paris.

MR. GOINEAU,

Head of the Personnel Department of the Schneider and Company Establishments.

MR. HENRY,

Chief Engineer of the Department of Rolling Stock and Traction of the P. L. M. Railway.

III.—*Workers' Delegate :*

MR. LEON JOUHAUX,
Secretary-General of the General Confederation of Labour.

Advisers :

MR. BIDEGARRAY,
Secretary of the Federation of Railway Workmen.

MLLE. JEANNE BOUVIER,
Member of the Federation of Clothing Workers.

MR. DUMOULIN,
Assistant Secretary of the General Confederation of Labour.

MR. LENOIR,
Secretary of the Federation of Metal Workers.

GREAT BRITAIN

I.—*Government Delegates :*

RT. HON. G. N. BARNES, M.P.,
Member of the War Cabinet.

SIR MALCOLM DELEVINGNE, K.C.B.,
Assistant Under Secretary of State—Home Office.

Advisers :

MR. G. BELLHOUSE,
Deputy Chief Inspector of Factories.

DR. T. M. LEGGE,
Senior Medical Inspector of Factories.

MISS CONSTANCE SMITH,
Senior Lady Inspector of Factories.

MR. I. H. MITCHELL,
Industrial Commissioner, Ministry of Labour.

MR. J. F. G. PRICE,
Assistant Secretary, Ministry of Labour.

II.—*Employers' Delegate :*

MR. D. S. MAJORIBANKS,
Managing Director, Sir W. G. Armstrong, Whitworth & Co., Ltd.

Advisers :

MR. G. S. MAGINNESS,
Assistant General Manager, Kynoch, Ltd.

DR. S. MIALL,
Director of the Brimsdown Lead Co.

MR. A. J. C. ROSS,
Managing Director of Hawthorne, Leslie &
Co., Ltd.

MR. HOWARD WILLIAMS,
Assistant General Manager of the London and
North Western Railway.

MRS. B. MAJORIBANKS,
Late Chief of the Employment Bureau for
Women at Sir W. G. Armstrong, Whitworth
& Co., Ltd.

III.—*Workers' Delegate :*

MR. G. H. STUART-BUNNING,
Ex-Chairman of the Parliamentary Committee,
Trades Union Congress.

Advisers :

RT. HON. C. W. BOWERMAN, M.P.,
Secretary, Parliamentary Committee, Trades
Union Congress.

MR. J. SEXTON, M.P.,
Transport Workers' Federation.

MR. T. SHAW, M.P., Weavers' Association.

MR. A. ONIONS, M.P., Miners' Federation.

MISS MARGARET BONDFIELD,
Member of the Parliamentary Committee,
Trades Union Congress.

MISS MARY MACARTHUR,
National Federation of Women Workers.

GREECE

I.—*Government Delegates :*

MR. JOHN SOFIANOPOULOS,
Assistant Secretary of the Ministry of National
Economy, First Delegate.

MR. ANGELUS SKINZOPOULOS,
Inspector of Industry of the Ministry of National
Economy, Second Delegate.

II.—*Employers' Delegate :*
    MR. EUGENE CANTACUZENE,
        Vice-President of the Greek Manufacturers'
        Association.

III.—*Workers' Delegate :*
    MR. TIMOLEON LAMPRINOPOULOS,
        Secretary, Workers' Federation, Pyræus.

GUATEMALA

I.—*Government Delegates :*
    MR. FRANCISCO SANCHEZ LATOUR,
        First Secretary of the Legation of Guatemala
        at Washington.
    DR. RAMON BENGOECHEA,
        Consul-General at New York.

II.—*Employers' Delegate :*
    MR. ALFREDO PALOMO RODRIGUEZ,
        Member of Parliament.

III.—*Workers' Delegate :*
    MR. MANUEL MORENO.

HAITI

Government Delegate :
    MR. CH. MORAVIA,
        Envoy Extraordinary and Minister Plenipo-
        tentiary.

INDIA

I.—*Government Delegates :*
    MR. LOUIS JAMES KERSHAW, C.S.I., C.I.E.,
        Secretary, Revenue and Statistics Dept., India
        Office, London.
    MR. ATUL CHANDRA CHATTERJEE, C.I.E.,
        I.C.S.,
        Acting Chief Secretary, United Provinces
        Government.

    Adviser :
    MR. JOHN DAVID FREDERICK ENGEL,
        Chief Inspector of Factories, Bombay Presi-
        dency.

II.—*Employers' Delegate :*
>MR. ALEXANDER ROBERTSON MURRAY,
>C.B.E.,
>>Chairman of the Indian Jute Mills Association.

III.—*Workers' Delegate :*
>MR. NARAYAN MALHAR JOSHI,
>>Secretary, Social Service League, Bombay.

>*Adviser :*
>MR. BAHMAN PESTONJI WADIA,
>>President, Madras Labour Union.

ITALY.
I.—*Government Delegates :*
>BARON MAYOR DES PLANCHES,
>>Senator and Ambassador.
>DR. G. DI PALMA CASTIGLIONE,
>>Royal Inspector of Emigration.

>*Advisers :*
>ING. BERNARDI,
>>Chief Inspector of Industries and Labour.
>ING. G. FASOLATO,
>>Inspector of Industries and Labour.
>MRS. CASARTELLI CABRINI,
>>General Secretary of Women's National Asso
>>ciation, Member of Central Committee of the
>>Employment Bureau.

II.—*Employers' Delegate :*
>COMM. E. BARONI,
>>President of Italian Union of Explosives
>>Manufacturers, replacing Ing. F. Quartieri,
>>President of the Italian Chemical Industry
>>Corp.

>*Adviser :*
>G. MYLIUS,
>>President of the Italian Cotton Association.

III.—*Workers' Delegate :*
>MR. GINO BALDESI,
>>Assistant Secretary-General of the Italian
>>General Confederation of Labour.

Advisers:
DR. MARIO SACCO,
  Counsellor to the Italian Confederation of Workers.
MR. GUIDO DI DIO,
  Assistant Secretary of the Federation of Metal Workers.

Interpreter:
MRS. OLIVIA ROSSETTI AGRESTI.

Secretary:
MISS ADRIANA VANZETTI.

JAPAN

I.—*Government Delegates:*
MR. EIKICHI KAMADA,
  President of Keio University, Member of the House of Peers.
DR. MINORU OKA,
  Ex-Director of the Bureau of Commerce and Industry of the Department of Agriculture and Commerce.

Advisers:
MR. SHOJI KONISHI,
  Expert Engineer of the Department of Commerce and Agriculture.
MR. TAKENORI KIKUCHI,
DR. YEIGORO KANASUGI,
  Member of the House of Representatives.
DR. KANJI KIGA,
  Member of the House of Representatives.
DR. TEIJIRO UYEDA,
  Professor of the Tokyo Commercial College.
MR. BUNJO KUBOTA,
MR. KYO KUMASAKI,
  Consul-General at New York.
DR. YAMATO ICHIHASHI,
  Professor of Leland Stanford Junior University, Cal.
MRS. TAKA TANAKA.

II.—*Employers' Delegate :*

> MR. SANJI MUTO,
>> Managing Director of the Kanegafuchi Spinning Co., Ltd.

> *Advisers :*

>> MR. ZENSUKE KUDO,
>>> Member of the House of Representatives.

>> MR. SHINKICHI TAMURA,
>>> President of the Chamber of Commerce, Kobe.

>> DR. RYUSAKU GODAI,
>>> Vice-President of the Mining Institute of Civil Engineers.

>> DR. SHOGO HASEGAWA,
>>> Managing Director of the Osaka Wagon Manufacturing Co., Ltd.

>> DR. IWASABURO NAKAHARA,
>>> President of the Japan Electric Association.

III.—*Workers' Delegate :*

> MR. UHEI MASUMOTO.

> *Advisers :*

>> MR. SHICHIRO MUTO,
>> MR. YEIJI OGASAWARA,
>> MR. KOHEI SATO,
>> MR. YOSHINARI KIDO,
>> MR. MAGOSABURO DOMAE.

NETHERLANDS

I.—*Government Delegates :*

> DR. W. H. NOLENS,
>> Member of the Second Chamber of the Netherlands Parliament ; Professor in Labour Legislation at Amsterdam University ; President of the Delegation.

> MR. G. J. VAN THIENEN,
>> Chief Inspector of Labour, Secretary of the Delegation.

> *Advisers :*

>> MRS. SUZE GROENEWEG,
>>> Member of the Second Chamber of the Netherlands Parliament.

>> MISS HENRIETTE KUYPER.

II.—*Employers' Delegate :*
>MR. J. A. E. VERKADE,
>>Vice-President of the Dutch Manufacturers' Association ; Member of the Industrial Council.

>*Advisers :*
>MR. S. TEN BOKKEL HUININK,
>>Contractor for Harbour Works, Member of the Town Council and Alderman of Ubbergen.
>MR. J. TER HAAR, Jr.,
>>Member of the Town Council of Amsterdam.
>MR. H. BLOMJOUS,
>>Manufacturer in Silburg, Member of the Industrial Council.

III.—*Workers' Delegate :*
>MR. J. OUDEGEEST,
>>Member of the Second Chamber of the Netherlands Parliament; President of the National Association of Labour Unions.

>*Advisers :*
>MR. P. SERRARENS,
>>Member of the Executive Council of the General Confederation of Catholic Trade Unions.
>MR. G. BAAS,
>>Vice-Secretary of the General Confederation of Christian Trade Unions.
>MR. B. HOLTROP,
>>President of the Netherlands Confederation of Trade Unions.

NICARAGUA.

>*Government Delegate :*
>SENOR DON RAMON ENRIQUEZ,
>>Consul-General at New Orleans, formerly Chargé d'Affaires at Washington, ex-Congressman.

NORWAY

I.—*Government Delegates :*
JUDGE JOHAN CASTBERG,
Ex-Minister of Labour, President of the Legislative Chamber of the Sorting.
JUDGE I. M. LUND,
Barrister at the Supreme Court, Mediator of the Kingdom.

Advisers :
MR. TH. G. THORSEN,
Secretary-General of the Ministry for Social Affairs.
MRS. BETZY KJELSBERG,
State Inspectress of Factories.

II.—*Employers' Delegate :*
MR. G. PAUS,
Sub-Director of the Association of Norwegian Employers.

III.—*Workers' Delegate :*
MR. J. TEIGEN,
Secretary-General of the Central Trade Union Organisation.

Advisers :
MR. J. VIDNES,
Member of Municipal Council of Christiania, Director of Publicity Bureau in the Department of Foreign Affairs.

Secretary of the Delegation :
MR. W. MORGENSTIERNE,
Commercial Counsellor of the Norwegian Legation at Washington.

PANAMA

I.—*Government Delegates :*
MR. JORGELUIS PAREDES,
MR. FEDERICO CALVO.

II.—*Employers' Delegate :*
MR. JOSE A. ZUBIETA.

III.—*Workers' Delegate :*
  MR. ANDRES MOJICA.

  Adviser :
  MR. JOSE E. LEFEVRE.

PARAGUAY

Government Delegates :
  DR. MANUEL GONDRA,
    Minister of Paraguay at Washington.
  MR. ARTURO CAMPOS,
    Director of Paraguayan Office of Money
    Exchange.

PERSIA

Government Delegates :
  MIRZA ADBUL ALI KHAN,
    Sadigh-es-Saltaneh, Envoy Extraordinary and
    Minister Plenipotentiary of Persia at Wash-
    ington.
  MIRZA ALI ASGHAR KHAN,
    Secretary of the Persian Legation at Wash-
    ington.

  Advisers :
  MR. HENRY C. FINKEL,
  MR. LOUIS ADDISON DENT.

PERU

I.—*Government Delegates :*
  MR. CARLOS PREVOST,
    Formerly Financial Agent for United States.
  MR. EDUARDO HIGGINSON,
    Consul-General of Peru to the United States.

II.—*Employers' Delegate :*
  MR. VICENTE GONZALES,
    National Society of Industries, Publisher,
    Journalist and Banker in New York City.

III.—*Workers' Delegate :*

  MR. VICTOR A. PUJAZON,
    Central International Union of Labourers.

  Adviser :
  MR. ALVAREZ DE BUENAVISTA.

POLAND

I.—*Government Delegates :*

  MR. FRANCSIZEK SOKAL,
    Director of Labour Department, Ministry of
    Labour and Social Welfare, President of the
    Polish Delegation to the International Labour
    Conference.
  MR. JOZEF RYMER,
    Member of Parliament, President of the Polish
    Workers' Union of Upper Silesia.

  Advisers :
  MRS. ZOFJA PRAUSSOWA,
    Labour Inspectress.
  MR. JAN ROGOWICZ,
  DR. WLADYSLAW-SOKOLOWSKI,
    Emigration Attaché to the United States.
  MR. MIECZYSLAW JASTRZEBOWSKI,
    Chief, Division of Labour, Employers' Associa-
    tion.
  MR. MACIEJ LASZCZYNSKI,
    Editor of " Labour's Voice."

II.—*Employers' Delegate :*

  MR. JAN ZAGLENICZNY,
    Formerly Minister of Trade and Commerce,
    President of the Labour Committee,
    Employers' Association.

III.—*Workers' Delegate :*

  MR. EDMUND BERNATOWICZ,
    President of the Polish Workers' Union.

PORTUGAL

I.—*Government Delegate:*
    MR. JOSÉ BARBOSA,
        Ex-Member of Parliament, President of the Court of Accounts.

    Advisers:
    MR. J. CAMOESAS,
        Member of Parliament.
    MR. THOMAS FERNANDEZ.

II.—*Employers' Delegate:*
    MR. ALVARO DE LAURDA,
        Acting President of the Commercial Association, Lisbon.

III.—*Workers' Delegate:*
    MR. ALFREDO FRANCO,
        President of the Committee for the Prevention of Unemployment.

ROUMANIA

    Government Delegates:
    MR. CONSTANTIN ORGHIDAN,
        Chief Engineer, Chief Inspector of Roumanian Railway Shops.
    MR. GREGORY MICHAESCO,
        Commercial Attaché, Legation of Roumania.

SAN DOMINGO

    Workers' Delegate:
    MR. T. E. KUNHARDT.

SERBS, CROATS, AND SLOVENES

I.—*Government Delegates:*
    DR. SLAVKO Y. GROUITCH,
        Envoy Extraordinary and Minister Plenipotentiary.
    DR. LUDEVIT PERITCH.

Advisers :
> MRS. MABEL GROUITCH,
> MR. VELIMIR STOYKOVITCH,
>> Inspector of Dept. of Commerce and Agriculture.

II.—*Employers' Delegate :*
> MR. MARKO BAUER,
>> Secretary of the Employers' Union, Zagreb.

III.—*Workers' Delegate :*
> MR. SVETA FRANTZ,
>> Secretary of the Labour Union of Ljubljana.

SIAM

Government Delegates :
> PHYA PRABHA KARAVONGSE,
>> Envoy Extraordinary and Minister Plenipo-
>> tentiary.
> PHYA CHANINDRA BHAKDI,
>> Secretary of the Legation of Siam at Wash-
>> ington.

SOUTH AFRICA

I.—*Government Delegate :*
> MR. H. WARINGTON SMYTH, C.M.G.,
>> Secretary for Mines and Industries and Acting
>> Chief Inspector of Factories.

II.—*Employers' Delegate :*
> MR. WILLIAM GEMMILL, F.I.A.,
>> Labour Adviser and Secretary and Actuary of
>> the Transvaal Diamond Mines.

III.—*Workers' Delegate :*
> MR. ARCHIBALD CRAWFORD,
>> Secretary of the South African Industrial Federa-
>> tion and of the South African Trade Union
>> Congress.

SPAIN

I.—*Government Delegates :*

VISCOUNT DE EZA, M.P.,
President of the National Institute for Social Reforms ; Ex-Minister of Industry, Commerce, Agriculture and Public Works ; President of the Spanish Delegation to the Conference.

MR. ADOLFO GONZALEZ POSADA,
Director in the National Institute for Social Reforms ; Professor of the Central University of Madrid ; Member of the Academy of Moral and Political Sciences ; Representative of the Spanish Government to the Conference.

Advisers :

MR. JOSE GASCON MARIN, M.P.,
Professor of the Central University of Madrid.

MARQUESA DE CASA CORTÉS.

MRS. TERESA ESCORIAZA,
Teacher, Ex-Pensionary of the Spanish Government.

MR. PEDRO SANGRO,
Assistant of the National Institute for Social Reforms ; Secretary of the Spanish Section of the International Association for the Protection of Labourers.

II.—*Employers' Delegate :*

MR. ALFONSO SALA, M.P.,
Honorary President of the Industrial Institute of Tarrasa ; Ex-Director-General of Commerce.

Advisers :

MR. ALFREDO RAMONEDA,
Employers' Mechanical and Chemical Engineer, President of the Association of Mechanical and Chemical Engineers of Barcelona.

MR. MIGUEL SASTRE.
Publicist.

III.—*Workers' Delegate :*

MR. FRANCISCO LARGO CABALLERO,
Member of the Board of National Institute for Social Reforms, Secretary of the General Workingmen's Union of Spain.

Advisers :

MR. FERNANDO DE LOS RIOS, M.P.,
Professor of the University of Granada.

MR. LUIS ARAQUISTAIN,
Publicist.

SWEDEN.

I.—*Government Delegates :*

JUDGE A. ERIK M. SJOBORG,
Minister Resident, Counsellor of the Legation of Sweden.

SENATOR R. G. HALFRED VON KOCH,
Chief Government Inspector of Charities.

Advisers :

DR. E. GUNNAR HUSS,
Bureau Chief and Acting President of Government Labour Board.

MISS KERSTIN HESSELGREN,
Government Inspectress of Factories.

II.—*Employers' Delegate :*

SENATOR HJALMAR VON SYDOW.
President of the Swedish Employers' Association.

Adviser :

DIR. J. SIGFRID EDSTROM,
President of the Federation of Mechanical Industries of Sweden.

III.—*Workers' Delegate :*

MR. A. HERMAN LINDQVIST,
Speaker, the Second Chamber of the Riksdag, President of Trade Unions Association.

Adviser :

MR. OTTO JOHANSSON,
Editor.

SWITZERLAND

I.—*Government Delegates :*
>   DR. HANS SULZER,
>   Swiss Minister at Washington.
>   DR. HERMANN RUFENACHT,
>   Director, Federal Office of Social Assurance at
>   Berne.
>   *Adviser :*
>   DR. HENRY WEGMANN,
>   Federal Inspector of Factories of the Third District at Zurich.

II.—*Employers' Delegate :*
>   MR. DIETRICH SCHINDLER,
>   Director-General of the Oerlikon Machine
>   Factory.

III.—*Workers' Delegate :*
>   MR. CONRAD ILG,
>   National Counsellor, Secretary of the Swiss
>   Federation of Metal and Clock Workers.

URUGUAY

Government Delegates :
>   DR. JACOBO VARELA,
>   Envoy Extraordinary and Minister Plenipotentiary at Washington.
>   MR. HUGO V. DE PEÑA,
>   Secretary-General.

VENEZUELA

I.—*Government Delegates :*
>   DR. DON SANTOS A. DOMINICI,
>   Envoy Extraordinary and Minister Plenipotentiary.
>   MR. NICOLAS VELOZ,
>   Consul-General at New Orleans.

APPENDIX III

DRAFT CONVENTIONS AND RECOMMENDATIONS

Adopted by the Conference at its First Annual Meeting,
October 29th-November 29th, 1919

I

DRAFT CONVENTION LIMITING THE HOURS OF WORK IN INDUSTRIAL UNDERTAKINGS TO EIGHT IN THE DAY AND FORTY-EIGHT IN THE WEEK

THE General Conference of the International Labour Organisation of the League of Nations,

Having been convened at Washington by the Government of the United States of America, on the 29th day of October, 1919, and

Having decided upon the adoption of certain proposals with regard to the " application of the principle of the 8-hours day or of the 48-hours week," which is the first item in the agenda for the Washington meeting of the Conference, and

Having determined that these proposals shall take the form of a draft international convention,

adopts the following Draft Convention for ratification by the Members of the International Labour Organisation, in accordance with the Labour Part of the Treaty of Versailles of June 28th, 1919, and of the Treaty of St. Germain of September 10th, 1919 :

ARTICLE 1

For the purpose of this Convention the term "industrial undertaking" includes particularly :

(*a*) Mines, quarries, and other works for the extraction of minerals from the earth.

(*b*) Industries in which articles are manufactured, altered, cleaned, repaired, ornamented, finished, adapted for sale, broken up or demolished, or in which materials are transformed ; including shipbuilding and the generation, transformation, and transmission of electricity or motive power of any kind.

(*c*) Construction, reconstruction, maintenance, repair, alteration, or demolition of any building, railway, tramway, harbour, dock, pier, canal, inland waterway, road, tunnel, bridge, viaduct, sewer, drain, well, telegraphic or telephonic installation, electrical undertaking, gaswork, waterwork or other work of construction, as well as the preparation for or laying the foundations of any such work or structure.

(*d*) Transport of passengers or goods by road, rail, sea or inland waterway, including the handling of goods at docks, quays, wharves or warehouses, but excluding transport by hand.

The provisions relative to transport by sea and on inland waterways shall be determined by a special conference dealing with employment at sea and on inland waterways.

The competent authority in each country shall define the line of division which separates industry from commerce and agriculture.

ARTICLE 2

The working hours of persons employed in any public or private industrial undertaking or in any branch thereof, other than an undertaking in which only members of the same family are employed, shall not exceed eight in the day and forty-eight in the week, with the exceptions hereinafter provided for.

(*a*) The provisions of this Convention shall not apply to persons holding positions of supervision or management, nor to persons employed in a confidential capacity.

(*b*) Where by law, custom or agreement between employers'

and workers' organisations, or, where no such organisations exist, between employers' and workers' representatives, the hours of work on one or more days of the week are less than eight, the limit of eight hours may be exceeded on the remaining days of the week by the sanction of the competent public authority, or by agreement between such organisations or representatives ; provided, however, that in no case under the provisions of this paragraph shall the daily limit of eight hours be exceeded by more than one hour.

(c) Where persons are employed in shifts it shall be permissible to employ persons in excess of eight hours in one day and forty-eight hours in any one week, if the average number of hours over a period of three weeks or less does not exceed eight per day and forty-eight per week.

ARTICLE 3

The limit of hours of work prescribed in Article 2 may be exceeded in case of accident, actual or threatened, or in case of urgent work to be done to machinery or plant, or in case of " force majeure," but only so far as may be necessary to avoid serious interference with the ordinary working of the undertaking.

ARTICLE 4

The limit of hours of work prescribed in Article 2 may also be exceeded in those processes which are required by reason of the nature of the process to be carried on continuously by a succession of shifts, subject to the condition that the working hours shall not exceed fifty-six in the week on the average. Such regulation of the hours of work shall in no case affect any rest days which may be secured by the national law to the workers in such processes in compensation for the weekly rest day.

ARTICLE 5

In exceptional cases where it is recognized that the provisions of Article 2 cannot be applied, but only in such cases, agreements between workers' and employers' organisations concerning the daily limit of work over a longer period of time may be given the force of regulations, if the Government, to which these agreements shall be submitted, so decides.

The average number of hours worked per week over the number of weeks covered by any such agreement shall not exceed forty-eight.

ARTICLE 6

Regulations made by public authority shall determine for industrial undertakings :

(a) The permanent exceptions that may be allowed in preparatory or complementary work which must necessarily be carried on outside the limits laid down for the general working of an establishment, or for certain classes of workers whose work is essentially intermittent.

(b) The temporary exceptions that may be allowed so that establishments may deal with exceptional cases of pressure of work.

These regulations shall be made only after consultation with the organisations of employers and workers concerned, if any such organisations exist. These regulations shall fix the maximum of additional hours in each instance, and the rate of pay for overtime shall not be less than one and one-quarter times the regular rate.

ARTICLE 7

Each Government shall communicate to the International Labour Office :

(a) A list of the processes which are classed as being necessarily continuous in character under Article 4 ;

(b) Full information as to working of the agreements mentioned in Article 5 ; and

(c) Full information concerning the regulations made under Article 6 and their application.

The International Labour Office shall make an annual report thereon to the General Conference of the International Labour Organisation.

ARTICLE 8

In order to facilitate the enforcement of the provisions of this Convention, every employer shall be required :

(*a*) To notify by means of the posting of notices in conspicuous places in the works or other suitable place, or by such other method as may be approved by the Government, the hours at which work begins and ends, and where work is carried on by shifts, the hours at which each shift begins and ends. These hours shall be so fixed that the duration of the work shall not exceed the limits prescribed by this Convention, and when so notified they shall not be changed except with such notice and in such manner as may be approved by the Government.

(*b*) To notify in the same way such rest intervals accorded during the period of work as are not reckoned as part of the working hours.

(*c*) To keep a record in the form prescribed by law or regulation in each country of all additional hours worked in pursuance of Articles 3 and 6 of this Convention.

It shall be made an offence against the law to employ any person outside the hours fixed in accordance with paragraph (*a*), or during the intervals fixed in accordance with paragraph (*b*).

ARTICLE 9

In the application of this Convention to Japan the following modifications and conditions shall obtain :

(*a*) The term " industrial undertaking " includes particularly—

The undertakings enumerated in paragraph (*a*) of Article 1 ;

The undertakings enumerated in paragraph (*b*) of Article 1, provided there are at least ten workers employed ;

The undertakings enumerated in paragraph (*c*) of Article 1, in so far as these undertakings shall be defined as " factories " by the competent authority ;

The undertakings enumerated in paragraph (*d*) of Article 1, except transport of passengers or goods by road, handling of goods at docks, quays, wharves, and warehouses, and transport by hand ; and,

Regardless of the number of persons employed, such of the undertakings enumerated in paragraphs (*b*) and (*c*) of Article 1 as may be declared by the competent authority either to be highly dangerous or to involve unhealthy processes.

(*b*) The actual working hours of persons of fifteen years of age or over in any public or private industrial undertaking, or in any branch thereof, shall not exceed fifty-seven in the week, except that in the raw-silk industry the limit may be sixty hours in the week.

(*c*) The actual working hours of persons under fifteen years of age in any public or private industrial undertaking, or in any branch thereof, and of all miners of whatever age engaged in underground work in the mines, shall in no case exceed forty-eight in the week.

(*d*) The limit of hours of work may be modified under the conditions provided for in Articles 2, 3, 4, and 5 of this Convention, but in no case shall the length of such modification bear to the length of the basic week a proportion greater than that which obtains in those Articles.

(*e*) A weekly rest period of twenty-four consecutive hours shall be allowed to all classes of workers.

(*f*) The provision in Japanese factory legislation limiting its application to places employing fifteen or more persons shall be amended so that such legislation shall apply to places employing ten or more persons.

(*g*) The provisions of the above paragraphs of this Article shall be brought into operation not later than July 1st, 1922, except that the provisions of Article 4 as modified by paragraph (*d*) of this Article shall be brought into operation not later than July 1st, 1923.

(*h*) The age of fifteen prescribed in paragraph (*c*) of this Article shall be raised, not later than July 1st, 1925, to sixteen.

ARTICLE 10

In British India the principle of a sixty-hour week shall be adopted for all workers in the industries at present covered by the Factory Acts administered by the Government of India, in mines, and in such branches of railway work as shall be specified for this purpose by the competent authority. Any modification of this limitation made by the competent authority shall be subject to the provisions of Articles 6 and 7 of this Convention. In other respects the provisions of this Convention shall not apply to India, but further provisions limiting the hours of work in India shall be considered at a future meeting of the General Conference.

ARTICLE 11

The provisions of this Convention shall not apply to China, Persia, and Siam, but provisions limiting the hours of work in these countries shall be considered at a future meeting of the General Conference.

ARTICLE 12

In the application of this Convention to Greece, the date at which its provisions shall be brought into operation in accordance with Article 19 may be extended to not later than July 1st, 1923, in the case of the following industrial undertakings :

    (1) Carbon-bisulphide works,
    (2) Acids works,
    (3) Tanneries,
    (4) Paper mills,
    (5) Printing works,
    (6) Sawmills,
    (7) Warehouses for the handling and preparation of tobacco,
    (8) Surface mining,
    (9) Foundries,
    (10) Lime works,
    (11) Dye works,
    (12) Glassworks (blowers),
    (13) Gas works (firemen),
    (14) Loading and unloading merchandise ;
and to not later than July 1st, 1924, in the case of the following industrial undertakings :

    (1) Mechanical industries : Machine shops for engines, safes, scales, beds, tacks, shells (sporting), iron foundries

bronze foundries, tin shops, plating shops, manufactories of hydraulic apparatus;

(2) Constructional industries: Limekilns, cement works, plasterers' shops, tile yards, manufactories of bricks and pavements, potteries, marble yards, excavating and building work;

(3) Textile industries: Spinning and weaving mills of all kinds, except dye works;

(4) Food industries: Flour and grist mills, bakeries, macaroni factories, manufactories of wines, alcohol and drinks, oil works, breweries, manufactories of ice and carbonated drinks, manufactories of confectioners' products and chocolate, manufactories of sausages and preserves, slaughter houses, and butcher shops;

(5) Chemical industries: Manufactories of synthetic colours, glassworks (except the blowers), manufactories of essence of turpentine and tartar, manufactories of oxygen and pharmaceutical products, manufactories of flaxseed oil, manufactories of glycerine, manufactories of calcium carbide, gas works (except the firemen);

(6) Leather industries: Shoe factories, manufactories of leather goods;

(7) Paper and printing industries; manufactories of envelopes, record books, boxes, bags, bookbinding, lithographing, and zinc-engraving shops;

(8) Clothing industries: Clothing shops, underwear and trimmings, workshops for pressing, workshops for bed coverings, artificial flowers, feathers and trimmings, hat and umbrella factories;

(9) Woodworking industries: Joiners' shops, coopers' sheds, wagon factories, manufactories of furniture and chairs, picture-framing establishments, brush and broom factories;

(10) Electrical industries: Power houses, shops for electrical installations;

(11) Transportation by land: Employees on railroads and street cars, firemen, drivers and carters.

ARTICLE 13[1]

In the application of this Convention to Roumania the date at which its provisions shall be brought into operation in accordance with Article 19 may be extended to not later than July 1st, 1924.

ARTICLE 14

The operation of the provisions of this Convention may be suspended in any country by the Government in the event of war or other emergency endangering the national safety.

ARTICLE 15

The formal ratifications of this Convention, under the conditions set forth in Part XIII of the Treaty of Versailles of June 28th, 1919, and of the Treaty of St. Germain of September 10th, 1919, shall be communicated to the Secretary-General of the League of Nations for registration.

ARTICLE 16

Each Member of the International Labour Organisation which ratifies this Convention engages to apply it to its colonies, protectorates and possessions which are not fully self-governing :

(*a*) Except where owing to the local conditions its provisions are inapplicable ; or

(*b*) Subject to such modifications as may be necessary to adapt its provisions to local conditions.

Each Member shall notify to the International Labour Office the action taken in respect of each of its colonies, protectorates and possessions which are not fully self-governing.

ARTICLE 17

As soon as the ratifications of two Members of the International Labour Organisation have been registered with the Secretariat, the Secretary-General of the League of Nations shall so notify all the Members of the International Labour Organisation.

ARTICLE 18

This Convention shall come into force at the date on which such notification is issued by the Secretary-General of the League of Nations, and it shall then be binding only upon those Members which have registered their ratifications with the Secretariat. Thereafter this Convention will come into force for any other Member at the date on which its ratification is registered with the Secretariat.

ARTICLE 19

Each Member which ratifies this Convention agrees to bring its provisions into operation not later than July 1st, 1921, and to take such action as may be necessary to make these provisions effective.

ARTICLE 20

A Member which has ratified this Convention may denounce it after the expiration of ten years from the date on which the Convention first comes into force, by an act communicated to the Secretary-General of the League of Nations for registration. Such denunciation shall not take effect until one year after the date on which it is registered with the Secretariat.

ARTICLE 21

At least once in ten years the Governing Body of the International Labour Office shall present to the General Conference a report on the working of this Convention, and shall consider the desirability of placing on the agenda of the Conference the question of its revision or modification.

ARTICLE 22

The French and English texts of this Convention shall both be authentic.

II.

DRAFT CONVENTION CONCERNING UNEMPLOYMENT.

The General Conference of the International Labour Organisation of the League of Nations,

> Having been convened at Washington by the Government of the United States of America, on the 29th day of October, 1919, and
>
> Having decided upon the adoption of certain proposals with regard to the " question of preventing or providing against unemployment," which is the second item in the agenda for the Washington meeting of the Conference, and
>
> Having determined that these proposals shall take the form of a draft international convention,

adopts the following Draft Convention for ratification by the Members of the International Labour Organisation, in accordance with the Labour Part of the Treaty of Versailles of June 28th, 1919, and of the Treaty of St. Germain of September 10th, 1919 :

ARTICLE 1

Each Member which ratifies this Convention shall communicate to the International Labour Office, at intervals as short as possible and not exceeding three months, all available information, statistical or otherwise, concerning unemployment, including reports on measures taken or contemplated to combat unemployment. Whenever practicable, the information shall be made available for such communication not later than three months after the end of the period to which it relates.

ARTICLE 2

Each Member which ratifies this Convention shall establish a system of free public employment agencies under the control of a central authority. Committees, which shall include representatives of employers and of workers, shall be appointed to advise on matters concerning the carrying on of these agencies.

Where both public and private free employment agencies exist, steps shall be taken to co-ordinate the operations of such agencies on a national scale.

The operations of the various national systems shall be co-ordinated by the International Labour Office in agreement with the countries concerned.

ARTICLE 3

The Members of the International Labour Organisation which ratify this Convention and which have established systems of insurance against unemployment shall, upon terms being agreed between the Members concerned, make arrangements whereby workers belonging to one Member and working in the territory of another shall be admitted to the same rates of benefit of such insurance as those which obtain for the workers belonging to the latter.

ARTICLE 4

The formal ratifications of this Convention, under the conditions set forth in Part XIII of the Treaty of Versailles of June 28th, 1919, and of the Treaty of St. Germain of September 10th, 1919, shall be communicated to the Secretary-General of the League of Nations for registration.

ARTICLE 5

Each Member of the International Labour Organisation which ratifies this Convention engages to apply it to its colonies, protectorates and possessions which are not fully self-governing :

(*a*) Except where owing to the local conditions its provisions are inapplicable ; or

(*b*) Subject to such modifications as may be necessary to adapt its provisions to local conditions.

Each Member shall notify to the International Labour Office the action taken in respect of each of its colonies, protectorates and possessions which are not fully self-governing.

12

ARTICLE 6

As soon as the ratifications of three Members of the International Labour Organisation have been registered with the Secretariat, the Secretary General of the League of Nations shall so notify all the Members of the International Labour Organisation.

ARTICLE 7

This Convention shall come into force at the date on which such notification is issued by the Secretary-General of the League of Nations, but it shall then be binding only upon those Members which have registered their ratifications with the Secretariat. Thereafter this Convention will come into force for any other Member at the date on which its ratification is registered with the Secretariat.

ARTICLE 8

Each Member which ratifies this Convention agrees to bring its provisions into operation not later than July 1st, 1921, and to take such action as may be necessary to make these provisions effective.

ARTICLE 9

A Member which has ratified this Convention may denounce it after the expiration of ten years from the date on which the Convention first comes into force, by an act communicated to the Secretary-General of the League of Nations for registration. Such denunciation shall not take effect until one year after the date on which it is registered with the Secretariat.

ARTICLE 10

At least once in ten years the Governing Body of the International Labour Office shall present to the General Conference a report on the working of this Convention, and shall consider the desirability of placing on the agenda of the Conference the question of its revision or modification.

ARTICLE 11

The French and English texts of this Convention shall both be authentic.

III

RECOMMENDATION CONCERNING UNEMPLOYMENT

The General Conference of the International Labour Organisation of the League of Nations,

> Having been convened at Washington by the Government of the United States of America on the 29th day of October, 1919, and
> Having decided upon the adoption of certain proposals with regard to the " question of preventing or providing against unemployment," which is the second item in the agenda for the Washington meeting of the Conference, and
> Having determined that these proposals shall take the form of a recommendation,

adopts the following Recommendation, to be submitted to the Members of the International Labour Organisation for consideration with a view to effect being given to it by national legislation or otherwise, in accordance with the Labour Part of the Treaty of Versailles of June 28th, 1919, and of the Treaty of St. Germain of September 10th, 1919 :

I

The General Conference recommends that each Member of the International Labour Organisation take measures to prohibit the establishment of employment agencies which charge fees or which carry on their business for profit. Where such agencies already exist, it is further recommended that they be permitted to operate only under Government licenses, and that all practicable measures be taken to abolish such agencies as soon as possible.

II

The General Conference recommends to the Members of the International Labour Organisation that the recruiting of bodies of workers in one country with a view to their employment in another country should be permitted only by mutual agreement between the countries concerned and after consultation with employers and workers in each country in the industries concerned.

III

The General Conference recommends that each Member of the International Labour Organisation establish an effective system of unemployment insurance, either through a Government system or through a system of Government subventions to associations whose rules provide for the payment of benefits to their unemployed members.

IV

The General Conference recommends that each Member of the International Labour Organisation co-ordinate the execution of all work undertaken under public authority, with a view to reserving such work as far as practicable for periods of unemployment and for districts most affected by it.

IV

RECOMMENDATION CONCERNING RECIPROCITY OF TREATMENT OF FOREIGN WORKERS.

The General Conference of the International Labour Organisation of the League of Nations,

Having been convened at Washington by the Government of the United States of America on the 29th day of October, 1919, and

Having decided upon the adoption of certain proposals with regard to the " question of preventing or providing against unemployment," which is the second item in the agenda for the Washington meeting of the Conference, and

Having determined that these proposals shall take the form of a recommendation,

adopts the following Recommendation to be submitted to the Members of the International Labour Organisation for consideration with a view to effect being given to it by national legislation or otherwise, in accordance with the Labour Part of the Treaty of Versailles of June 28th, 1919, and of the Treaty of St. Germain of September 10th, 1919 :

The General Conference recommends that each Member of the International Labour Organisation shall, on condition of reciprocity and upon terms to be agreed between the countries concerned, admit the foreign workers (together with their families) employed within its territory to the benefit of its laws and regulations for the protection of its own workers, as well as to the right of lawful organisation as enjoyed by its own workers.

V

DRAFT CONVENTION CONCERNING THE EMPLOYMENT OF WOMEN BEFORE AND AFTER CHILDBIRTH

The General Conference of the International Labour Organisation of the League of Nations,

Having been convened at Washington by the Government of the United States of America on the 29th day of October, 1919, and

Having decided upon the adoption of certain proposals with regard to " women's employment before and after childbirth, including the question of maternity benefit," which is part of the third item in the agenda for the Washington meeting of the Conference, and

Having determined that these proposals shall take the form of a draft international convention,

adopts the following Draft Convention for ratification by the

Members of the International Labour Organisation, in accordance with the Labour Part of the Treaty of Versailles of June 28th, 1919, and of the Treaty of St. Germain of September 10th, 1919:

ARTICLE 1

For the purpose of this Convention, the term " industrial undertaking " includes particularly :

(*a*) Mines, quarries and other works for the extraction of minerals from the earth.

(*b*) Industries in which articles are manufactured, altered, cleaned, repaired, ornamented, finished, adapted for sale, broken up or demolished, or in which materials are transformed ; including shipbuilding and the generation, transformation, and transmission of electricity or motive power of any kind.

(*c*) Construction, reconstruction, maintenance, repair, alteration or demolition of any building, railway, tramway, harbour, dock, pier, canal, inland waterway, road, tunnel, bridge, viaduct, sewer, drain, well, telegraphic or telephonic installation, electrical undertaking, gaswork, waterwork or other work of construction, as well as the preparation for or laying the foundation of any such work or structure.

(*d*) Transport of passengers or goods by road, rail, sea or inland waterway, including the handling of goods at docks, quays, wharves and warehouses but excluding transport by hand.

For the purpose of this Convention, the term " commercial undertaking " includes any place where articles are sold or where commerce is carried on.

The competent authority in each country shall define the line of division which separates industry and commerce from agriculture.

ARTICLE 2

For the purpose of this Convention the term " woman " signifies any female person, irrespective of age or nationality, whether married or unmarried, and the term " child " signifies any child whether legitimate or illegitimate.

ARTICLE 3

In any public or private industrial or commercial under-taking, or in any branch thereof, other than an undertaking in which only members of the same family are employed, a woman—

(*a*) Shall not be permitted to work during the six weeks following her confinement.

(*b*) Shall have the right to leave her work if she produces a medical certificate stating that her confinement will probably take place within six weeks.

(*c*) Shall, while she is absent from her work in pursuance of paragraphs (*a*) and (*b*) be paid benefits sufficient for the full and healthy maintenance of herself and her child, provided either out of public funds or by means of a system of insurance, the exact amount of which shall be determined by the competent authority in each country, and as an additional benefit shall be entitled to free attendance by a doctor or certified midwife. No mistake of the medical adviser in estimating the date of confinement shall preclude a woman from receiving these benefits from the date of the medical certificate up to the date on which the confinement actually takes place.

(*d*) Shall in any case, if she is nursing her child, be allowed half an hour twice a day during her working hours for this purpose.

ARTICLE 4

Where a woman is absent from her work in accordance with paragraphs (*a*) or (*b*) of Article 3 of this Convention, or remains absent from her work for a longer period as a result of illness medically certified to arise out of pregnancy or confinement and rendering her unfit for work, it shall not be lawful, until her absence shall have exceeded a maximum period to be fixed by the competent authority in each country, for her employer to give her notice of dismissal during such absence, nor to give her notice of dismissal at such a time that the notice would expire during such absence.

ARTICLE 5

The formal ratifications of this Convention, under the

conditions set forth in Part XIII of the Treaty of Versailles of June 28th, 1919, and of the Treaty of St. Germain of September 10th, 1919, shall be communicated to the Secretary-General of the League of Nations for registration.

ARTICLE 6

Each Member of the International Labour Organisation which ratifies this Convention engages to apply it to its colonies, protectorates and possessions which are not fully self-governing :

(*a*) Except where, owing to the local conditions, its provisions are inapplicable ; or

(*b*) Subject to such modifications as may be necessary to adapt its provisions to local conditions.

Each Member shall notify to the International Labour Office the action taken in respect of each of its colonies, protectorates and possessions which are not fully self-governing.

ARTICLE 7

As soon as the ratifications of two Members of the International Labour Organisation have been registered with the Secretariat, the Secretary-General of the League of Nations shall so notify all the Members of the International Labour Organisation.

ARTICLE 8

This Convention shall come into force at the date on which such notification is issued by the Secretary-General of the League of Nations, but it shall then be binding only upon those Members which have registered their ratifications with the Secretariat. Thereafter this Convention will come into force for any other Member at the date on which its ratification is registered with the Secretariat.

ARTICLE 9

Each Member which ratifies this Convention agrees to bring its provisions into operation not later than July 1st, 1922, and to take such action as may be necessary to make these provisions effective.

ARTICLE 10

A Member which has ratified this Convention may denounce it after the expiration of ten years from the date on which the Convention first comes into force, by an act communicated to the Secretary-General of the League of Nations for registration. Such denunciation shall not take effect until one year after the date on which it is registered with the Secretariat.

ARTICLE 11

At least once in ten years the Governing Body of the International Labour Office shall present to the General Conference a report on the working of this Convention, and shall consider the desirability of placing on the agenda of the Conference the question of its revision or modification.

ARTICLE 12

The French and English texts of this Convention shall both be authentic.

VI

DRAFT CONVENTION CONCERNING EMPLOYMENT OF WOMEN DURING THE NIGHT

The General Conference of the International Labour Organisation of the League of Nations,

Having been convened at Washington by the Government of the United States of America, on the 29th day of October, 1919, and

Having decided upon the adoption of certain proposals with regard to "women's employment during the night," which is part of the third item in the agenda for the Washington meeting of the Conference, and

Having determined that these proposals shall take the form of a draft international convention,

adopts the following Draft Convention for ratification by the Members of the International Labour Organisation, in accordance with the Labour Part of the Treaty of Versailles of June 28th, 1919, and of the Treaty of St. Germain of September 10th, 1919 :

ARTICLE 1

For the purpose of this Convention, the term " industrial undertaking " includes particularly :

(a) Mines, quarries and other works for the extraction of minerals from the earth ;

(b) Industries in which articles are manufactured, altered, cleaned, repaired, ornamented, finished, adapted for sale, broken up or demolished, or in which materials are transformed ; including shipbuilding, and the generation, transformation, and transmission of electricity or motive power of any kind ;

(c) Construction, reconstruction, maintenance, repair, alteration or demolition of any building, railway, tramway, harbour, dock, pier, canal, inland waterway, road, tunnel, bridge, viaduct, sewer, drain, well, telegraphic or telephonic installation, electrical undertaking, gaswork, waterwork or other work of construction, as well as the preparation for or laying the foundations of any such work or structure.

The competent authority in each country shall define the line of division which separates industry from commerce and agriculture.

ARTICLE 2

For the purpose of this Convention, the term " night " signifies a period of at least eleven consecutive hours, including the interval between ten o'clock in the evening and five o'clock in the morning.

In those countries where no Government regulation as yet applies to the employment of women in industrial undertakings during the night, the term " night " may provisionally, and for a maximum period of three years, be declared by the Government to signify a period of only ten hours, including the interval between ten o'clock in the evening and five o'clock in the morning.

ARTICLE 3

Women without distinction of age shall not be employed during the night in any public or private industrial undertaking, or in any branch thereof, other than an undertaking in which only members of the same family are employed.

ARTICLE 4

Article 3 shall not apply :

(*a*) In cases of "force majeure," when in any undertaking there occurs an interruption of work which it was impossible to foresee, and which is not of a recurring character.

(*b*) In cases where the work has to do with raw materials, or materials in course of treatment which are subject to rapid deterioration, when such night work is necessary to preserve the said materials from certain loss.

ARTICLE 5

In India and Siam the application of Article 3 of this Convention may be suspended by the Government in respect to any industrial undertaking, except factories as defined by the national law. Notice of every such suspension shall be filed with the International Labour Office.

ARTICLE 6

In industrial undertakings which are influenced by the seasons, and in all cases where exceptional circumstances demand it, the night period may be reduced to ten hours on sixty days of the year.

ARTICLE 7

In countries where the climate renders work by day particularly trying to the health, the night period may be shorter than prescribed in the above articles, provided that compensatory rest is accorded during the day.

ARTICLE 8

The formal ratifications of this Convention, under the conditions set forth in Part XIII of the Treaty of Versailles of June 28th, 1919, and of the Treaty of St. Germain of September 10th, 1919, shall be communicated to the Secretary-General of the League of Nations for registration.

ARTICLE 9

Each Member of the International Labour Organisation which ratifies this Convention engages to apply it to its colonies, protectorates and possessions which are not fully self-governing :

(a) Except where owing to the local conditions its provisions are inapplicable ; or

(b) Subject to such modifications as may be necessary to adapt its provisions to local conditions.

Each Member shall notify to the International Labour Office the action taken in respect of each of its colonies, protectorates and possessions which are not fully self-governing.

ARTICLE 10

As soon as the ratifications of two Members of the International Labour Organisation have been registered with the Secretariat, the Secretary-General of the League of Nations shall so notify all the Members of the International Labour Organisation.

ARTICLE 11

This Convention shall come into force at the date on which such notification is issued by the Secretary-General of the League of Nations, but it shall then be binding only upon those Members which have registered their ratifications with the Secretariat. Thereafter this Convention will come into force for any other Member at the date on which its ratification is registered with the Secretariat.

ARTICLE 12

Each Member which ratifies this Convention agrees to bring its provisions into operation not later than July 1st, 1922, and to take such action as may be necessary to make these provisions effective.

ARTICLE 13

A Member which has ratified this Convention may denounce it after the expiration of ten years from the date on which the Convention first comes into force, by an act communicated to the Secretary-General of the League of Nations for registration. Such denunciation shall not take effect until one year after the date on which it is registered with the Secretariat.

ARTICLE 14

At least once in ten years the Governing Body of the International Labour Office shall present to the General Conference a report on the working of this Convention, and shall consider the desirability of placing on the agenda of the Conference the question of its revision or modification.

ARTICLE 15

The French and English texts of this Convention shall both be authentic.

VII

RECOMMENDATION CONCERNING THE PREVENTION OF ANTHRAX

The General Conference of the International Labour Organisation of the League of Nations,

Having been convened at Washington by the Government of the United States of America on the 29th day of October, 1919, and

Having decided upon the adoption of certain proposals with regard to " women's employment : unhealthy processes," which is part of the third item in the agenda for the Washington meeting of the Conference ; and

Having determined that these proposals shall take the form of a recommendation,

adopts the following Recommendation, to be submitted to the Members of the International Labour Organisation for consideration with a view to effect being given to it by national legislation or otherwise, in accordance with the Labour Part of the Treaty of Versailles of June 28th, 1919, and the Treaty of St. Germain of September 10th, 1919 :

The General Conference recommends to the Members of the International Labour Organisation that arrangements should be made for the disinfection of wool infected with anthrax spores, either in the country exporting such wool, or, if that is not practicable, at the port of entry in the country importing such wool.

VIII

RECOMMENDATION CONCERNING THE PROTEC-TION OF WOMEN AND CHILDREN AGAINST LEAD POISONING

The General Conference of the International Labour Organisation of the League of Nations,

Having been convened at Washington by the Government of the United States of America on the 29th day of October, 1919, and

Having decided upon the adoption of certain proposals with regard to " women's and children's employment : unhealthy processes," which is part of the third and fourth items in the agenda for the Washington meeting of the Conference, and

Having determined that these proposals shall take the form of a recommendation,

adopts the following Recommendation, to be submitted to the Members of the International Labour Organisation for consideration with a view to effect being given to it by national legislation or otherwise, in accordance with the Labour Part of the Treaty of Versailles of June 28th, 1919, and of the Treaty of St. Germain of September 10th, 1919 :

The General Conference recommends to the Members of the International Labour Organisation that in view of the danger involved to the function of maternity and to the physical development of children, women and young persons under the age of eighteen years be excluded from employment in the following processes :

(a) In furnace work in the reduction of zinc or lead ores.

(b) In the manipulation, treatment or reduction of ashes containing lead, and in the desilverizing of lead.

(c) In melting lead or old zinc on a large scale.

(d) In the manufacture of solder or alloys containing more than ten per cent. of lead.

(e) In the manufacture of litharge, massicot, red lead, white lead, orange lead, or sulphate, chromate or silicate (frit) of lead.

(f) In mixing and pasting in the manufacture or repair of electric accumulators.

(g) In the cleaning of workrooms where the above processes are carried on.

It is further recommended that the employment of women and young persons under the age of eighteen years in processes involving the use of lead compounds be permitted only subject to the following conditions :

(a) Locally applied exhaust ventilation, so as to remove dust and fumes at the point of origin.

(b) Cleanliness of tools and workrooms.

(c) Notification to Government authorities of all cases of lead poisoning, and compensation therefor.

(d) Periodic medical examination of the persons employed in such processes.

(e) Provision of sufficient and suitable cloakroom, washing, and messroom accommodation, and of special protective clothing.

(f) Prohibition of bringing food or drink into workrooms.

It is further recommended that in industries where soluble lead compounds can be replaced by non-toxic substances, the use of soluble lead compounds should be strictly regulated

For the purpose of this Recommendation, a lead compound should be considered as soluble if it contains more than five per cent. of its weight (estimated as metallic lead) soluble in a quarter of one per cent. solution of hydrochloric acid.

IX

RECOMMENDATION CONCERNING THE ESTAB-LISHMENT OF GOVERNMENT HEALTH SER-VICES

The General Conference of the International Labour Organisation of the League of Nations,

> Having been convened at Washington by the Government of the United States of America on the 29th day of October, 1919, and
> Having decided upon the adoption of certain proposals with regard to " women's employment : unhealthy processes," which is part of the third item in the agenda for the Washington meeting of the Conference, and
> Having determined that these proposals shall take the form of a recommendation,

adopts the following Recommendation, to be submitted to the Members of the International Labour Organisation for consideration with a view to effect being given to it by national legislation or otherwise, in accordance with the Labour Part of the Treaty of Versailles of June 28th, 1919, and the Treaty of St. Germain of September 10th, 1919 :

The General Conference recommends that each Member of the International Labour Organisation which has not already done so should establish as soon as possible, not only a system of efficient factory inspection, but also in addition thereto a Government service especially charged with the duty of safeguarding the health of the workers, which will keep in touch with the International Labour Office.

X

DRAFT CONVENTION FIXING THE MINIMUM AGE FOR ADMISSION OF CHILDREN TO INDUSTRIAL EMPLOYMENT

The General Conference of the International Labour Organisation of the League of Nations,

Having been convened by the Government of the United States of America at Washington, on the 29th day of October, 1919, and

Having decided upon the adoption of certain proposals with regard to the " employment of children : minimum age of employment," which is part of the fourth item in the agenda for the Washington meeting of the Conference, and

Having determined that these proposals shall take the form of a draft international convention,

adopts the following Draft Convention for ratification by the Members of the International Labour Organisation, in accordance with the Labour Part of the Treaty of Versailles of June 28th, 1919, and of the Treaty of St. Germain of September 10th, 1919 :

<h3 align="center">Article i</h3>

For the purpose of this Convention, the term "industrial undertaking " includes particularly :

(*a*) Mines, quarries and other works for the extraction of minerals from the earth.

(*b*) Industries in which articles are manufactured, altered, cleaned, repaired, ornamented, finished, adapted for sale, broken up or demolished, or in which materials are transformed ; including shipbuilding, and the generation, transformation and transmission of electricity and motive power of any kind.

(*c*) Construction, reconstruction, maintenance, repair, alteration or demolition of any building, railway, tramway, harbour, dock, pier, canal, inland waterway, road, tunnel, bridge, viaduct, sewer, drain, well, telegraphic or telephonic installation, electrical undertaking, gaswork, waterwork or other work of construction, as well as the preparation for or laying the foundations of any such work or structure.

(*d*) Transport of passengers or goods by road or rail or inland waterway, including the handling of goods at docks, quays, wharves and warehouses, but excluding transport by hand.

The competent authority in each country shall define the line of division which separates industry from commerce and agriculture.

13

ARTICLE 2

Children under the age of fourteen years shall not be employed or work in any public or private industrial undertaking, or in any branch thereof, other than an undertaking in which only members of the same family are employed.

ARTICLE 3

The provisions of Article 2 shall not apply to work done by children in technical schools, provided that such work is approved and supervised by public authority.

ARTICLE 4

In order to facilitate the enforcement of the provisions of this Convention, every employer in an industrial undertaking shall be required to keep a register of all persons under the age of sixteen years employed by him, and of the dates of their births.

ARTICLE 5

In connexion with the application of this Convention to Japan, the following modifications of Article 2 may be made :

(*a*) Children over twelve years of age may be admitted into employment if they have finished the course in the elementary school ;

(*b*) As regards children between the ages of twelve and fourteen already employed, transitional regulations may be made.

The provision in the present Japanese law admitting children under the age of twelve years to certain light and easy employments shall be repealed.

ARTICLE 6

The provisions of Article 2 shall not apply to India, but in India children under twelve years of age shall not be employed,

(*a*) In manufactories working with power and employing more than ten persons ;

(*b*) In mines, quarries, and other works for the extraction of minerals from the earth ;

(*c*) In the transport of passengers or goods, or mails, by rail, or in the handling of goods at docks, quays and wharves, but excluding transport by hand.

ARTICLE 7

The formal ratifications of this Convention, under the conditions set forth in Part XIII of the Treaty of Versailles of June 28th, 1919, and of the Treaty of St. Germain of September 10th, 1919, shall be communicated to the Secretary-General of the League of Nations for registration.

ARTICLE 8

Each Member of the International Labour Organisation which ratifies this Convention engages to apply it to its colonies, protectorates and possessions which are not fully self-governing :

(*a*) Except where owing to the local conditions its provisions are inapplicable ; or

(*b*) Subject to such modifications as may be necessary to adapt its provisions to local conditions.

Each Member shall notify to the International Labour Office the action taken in respect to each of its colonies, protectorates and possessions which are not fully self-governing.

ARTICLE 9

As soon as the ratifications of two Members of the International Labour Organisation have been registered with the Secretariat, the Secretary-General of the League of Nations shall so notify all the members of the International Labour Organisation.

ARTICLE 10

This Convention shall come into force at the date on which such notification is issued by the Secretary-General of the League of Nations, but it shall then be binding only upon those Members which have registered their ratifications with the Secretariat. Thereafter this Convention will come into force for any other Member at the date on which its ratification is registered with the Secretariat.

ARTICLE 11

Each Member which ratifies this Convention agrees to bring its provisions into operation not later than July 1st, 1922, and to take such action as may be necessary to make these provisions effective.

ARTICLE 12

A Member which has ratified this Convention may denounce it after the expiration of ten years from the date on which the Convention first comes into force, by an act communicated to the Secretary-General of the League of Nations for registration. Such denunciation shall not take effect until one year after the date on which it is registered with the Secretariat.

ARTICLE 13

At least once in ten years the Governing Body of the International Labour Office shall present to the General Conference a report on the working of this Convention, and shall consider the desirability of placing on the agenda of the Conference the question of its revision or modification.

ARTICLE 14

The French and English texts of this Convention shall both be authentic.

XI

DRAFT CONVENTION CONCERNING THE NIGHT WORK OF YOUNG PERSONS EMPLOYED IN INDUSTRY

The General Conference of the International Labour Organisation of the League of Nations,

Having been convened by the Government of the United States of America at Washington, on the 29th day of October, 1919, and

Having decided upon the adoption of certain proposals

with regard to the " employment of children during the night," which is part of the fourth item in the agenda for the Washington meeting of the Conference, and

Having determined that these proposals shall take the form of a draft international convention,

adopts the following Draft Convention for ratification by the Members of the International Labour Organisation, in accordance with the Labour Part of the Treaty of Versailles June 28th, 1919, and of the Treaty of St. Germain of September 10th, 1919 :

ARTICLE 1

For the purpose of this Convention, the term " industrial undertaking " includes particularly :

(a) Mines, quarries, and other works for the extraction of minerals from the earth.

(b) Industries in which articles are manufactured, altered, cleaned, repaired, ornamented, finished, adapted for sale, broken up or demolished, or in which materials are transformed ; including shipbuilding, and the generation, transformation and transmission of electricity or motive power of any kind.

(c) Construction, reconstruction, maintenance, repair, alteration or demolition of any building, railway, tramway, harbour, dock, pier, canal, inland waterway or telephonic installation, electrical undertaking, gaswork, waterwork or other work of construction as well as the preparation for or laying the foundations of any such work or structure.

(d) Transport of passengers or goods by road or rail, including the handling of goods at docks, quays, wharves and warehouses, but excluding transport by hand.

The competent authority in each country shall define the line of division which separates industry from commerce and agriculture.

ARTICLE 2

Young persons under eighteen years of age shall not be employed during the night in any public or private industrial undertaking, or in any branch thereof, other than an undertaking in which only members of the same family are employed, except as hereinafter provided for.

Young persons over the age of sixteen may be employed during the night in the following industrial undertakings on work which by reason of the nature of the process is required to be carried on continuously day and night :

(*a*) Manufacture of iron and steel ; processes in which reverberatory or regenerative furnaces are used, and galvanizing of sheet metal or wire (except the pickling process).

(*b*) Glass works.

(*c*) Manufacture of paper.

(*d*) Manufacture of raw sugar.

(*e*) Gold mining reduction work.

ARTICLE 3

For the purpose of this Convention, the term " night " signifies a period of at least eleven consecutive hours, including the interval between ten o'clock in the evening and five o'clock in the morning.

In coal and lignite mines work may be carried on in the interval between ten o'clock in the evening and five o'clock in the morning, if an interval of ordinarily fifteen hours, and in no case of less than thirteen hours, separates two periods of work.

Where night work in the baking industry is prohibited for all workers, the interval between nine o'clock in the evening and four o'clock in the morning may be substituted in the baking industry for the interval between ten o'clock in the evening and five o'clock in the morning.

In those tropical countries in which work is suspended during the middle of the day, the night period may be shorter than eleven hours if compensatory rest is accorded during the day.

ARTICLE 4

The provisions of Articles 2 and 3 shall not apply to the night work of young persons between the ages of sixteen and eighteen years in cases of emergencies which could not have been controlled or foreseen, which are not of a periodical character, and which interfere with the normal working of the industrial undertaking.

ARTICLE 5

In the application of this Convention to Japan, until July 1st, 1925, Article 2 shall apply only to young persons under fifteen years of age, and thereafter it shall apply only to young persons under sixteen years of age.

ARTICLE 6

In the application of this Convention to India, the term "industrial undertaking" shall include only "factories" as defined in the Indian Factory Act, and Article 2 shall not apply to male young persons over fourteen years of age.

ARTICLE 7

The prohibition of night work may be suspended by the Government, for young persons between the ages of sixteen and eighteen years, when in case of serious emergency the public interest demands it.

ARTICLE 8

The formal ratifications of this Convention, under the conditions set forth in Part XIII of the Treaty of Versailles of June 28th, 1919, and of the Treaty of St. Germain of September 10th, 1919, shall be communicated to the Secretary-General of the League of Nations for registration.

ARTICLE 9

Each Member of the International Labour Organisation which ratifies this Convention engages to apply it to its colonies, protectorates and possessions which are not fully self-governing :

(a) Except where owing to the local conditions its provisions are inapplicable ; or

(b) Subject to such modifications as may be necessary to adapt its provisions to local conditions.

Each Member shall notify to the International Labour

Office the action taken in respect of each of its colonies, protectorates and possessions which are not fully self-governing.

ARTICLE 10

As soon as the ratifications of two Members of the International Labour Organisation have been registered with the Secretariat the Secretary-General of the League of Nations shall so notify all the Members of the International Labour Organisation.

ARTICLE 11

This Convention shall come into force at the date on which such notification is issued by the Secretary-General of the League of Nations, and it shall then be binding only upon those Members which have registered their ratifications with the Secretariat. Thereafter this Convention will come into force for any other Member at the date on which its ratification is registered with the Secretariat.

ARTICLE 12

Each Member which ratifies this Convention agrees to bring its provisions into operation not later than July 1st, 1922, and to take such action as may be necessary to make these provisions effective.

ARTICLE 13

A Member which has ratified this Convention may denounce it after the expiration of ten years from the date on which the Convention first comes into force, by an act communicated to the Secretary-General of the League of Nations for registration. Such denunciation shall not take effect until one year after the date on which it is registered with the Secretariat.

ARTICLE 14

At least once in ten years the Governing Body of the International Labour Office shall present to the General Conference a report on the working of this Convention, and shall consider the desirability of placing on the agenda of the Conference the question of its revision or modification.

ARTICLE 15

The French and English texts of this Convention shall both be authentic.

XII

RECOMMENDATION CONCERNING THE APPLICATION OF THE BERNE CONVENTION OF 1906, ON THE PROHIBITION OF THE USE OF WHITE PHOSPHORUS IN THE MANUFACTURE OF MATCHES

The General Conference of the International Labour Organisation of the League of Nations,

> Having been convened at Washington by the Government of the United States of America on the 29th day of October, 1919, and
> Having decided upon the adoption of a proposal with regard to the " extension and application of the International Convention adopted at Berne in 1906 on the prohibition of the use of white phosphorus in the manufacture of matches," which is part of the fifth item in the agenda for the Washington meeting of the Conference, and
> Having determined that this proposal shall take the form of a Recommendation,

adopts the following Recommendation, to be submitted to the Members of the International Labour Organisation for consideration with a view to effect being given to it by national legislation or otherwise, in accordance with the Labour Part of the Treaty of Versailles of June 28th, 1919, and the Treaty of St. Germain of September 10th, 1919 :

The General Conference recommends that each Member of the International Labour Organisation, which has not already done so, should adhere to the International Convention adopted at Berne in 1906 on the prohibition of the use of white phosphorus in the manufacture of matches.

APPENDIX IV

GOVERNING BODY OF THE INTERNATIONAL LABOUR OFFICE

MR. ARTHUR FONTAINE (France : Government), *Chairman.*
MR. F. A. ACLAND (Canada : Government).
MR. DE ALVEAR (Argentine : Government).
MR. G. H. STUART-BUNNING (Great Britain : Workers).
MR. J. CARLIER (Belgium : Employers).
SIR MALCOLM DELEVINGNE, K.C.B. (Great Britain : Government).
MR. P. M. DRAPER (Canada : Workers).
VICOMTE DE EZA (Spain : Government).
MR. L. GUÉRIN (France : Employers).
MR. F. HODACZ (Czecho-Slovakia : Employers).
MR. L. JOUHAUX (France : Workers).
MR. K. LEGIEN (Germany : Workers).
DR. LEYMANN (Germany : Government).
MR. H. LINDQUIST (Sweden : Workers).
MR. E. MAHAIM (Belgium : Government).
BARON MAYOR DES PLANCHES (Italy : Government).
MR. NAGAOKA (Japan : Government).
MR. J. OUDEGEEST (Holland : Workers).
MR. A. PIRELLI (Italy : Employers).
MR. H. RÜFENACHT (Switzerland : Government).
MR. D. SCHINDLER (Switzerland : Employers).
MR. F. SOKAL (Poland : Government).
SIR ALLAN SMITH (Great Britain : Employers).
DR. VEDEL (Denmark : Government).

POSTSCRIPT

It may be of interest if the following notes are added :

(1) Action of the British Government on the Washington Conventions :

- (a) *Hours of Work.* A Forty-eight Hours' Bill has been drafted; but owing to difficulties as to the inclusion of agricultural workers and seamen, it is at present in suspense.
- (b) *Unemployment.* The system at present in operation in Great Britain covers the main part of the Convention on this subject, though there are certain points such as the co-ordination of public and private employment exchanges, which are not covered. No steps appear to have been taken to ratify this convention.
- (c) *Employment of Women before and after Childbirth.* The Ministry of Health is understood to be preparing a draft of a Bill on this subject.
- (d) *Employment of Women and Children during the night ; and age of admission of Children to Industry.* These questions are covered by the Women, Young Persons and Children Employment Bill, which is already before the House of Commons. A good deal of difficulty has been caused by the insertion in the Bill of some more or less irrelevant provisions, to which the Labour Party strongly objects.

(2) The Genoa Conference.

The Conference has just finished its session ; and there s no material available except somewhat scanty newspaper eports. The meeting appears to have been more stormy and o have gone through more acute crises than the Washington Conference experienced. Unfortunately, great changes were made in the composition of delegations—the British delegates in particular, including no one who had been at Washington.

The main business of the Conference was the application of the Washington Conventions to seamen. The most important Convention—that on Hours of Work—failed, by one vote, to get the necessary two-thirds majority. The British Government and Employers' delegates are reported to have voted in the successful minority. Some of the other Conventions were adopted, notably those dealing with unemployment and with the prohibition of the employment of children.

INDEX

Printed in Great Britain by Jarrold & Sons, Ltd., Norwich

A SELECTION FROM
MESSRS. METHUEN'S
PUBLICATIONS

This Catalogue contains only a selection of the more important books published by Messrs. Methuen. A complete catalogue of their publications may be obtained on application.

Bain (F. W.)—
A DIGIT OF THE MOON: A Hindoo Love Story. THE DESCENT OF THE SUN: A Cycle of Birth. A HEIFER OF THE DAWN. IN THE GREAT GOD'S HAIR. A DRAUGHT OF THE BLUE. AN ESSENCE OF THE DUSK. AN INCARNATION OF THE SNOW. A MINE OF FAULTS. THE ASHES OF A GOD. BUBBLES OF THE FOAM. A SYRUP OF THE BEES. THE LIVERY OF EVE. THE SUB-STANCE OF A DREAM. *All Fcap. 8vo. 5s. net.* AN ECHO OF THE SPHERES. *Wide Demy. 12s. 6d. net.*

Balfour (Graham). THE LIFE OF ROBERT LOUIS STEVENSON. *Fifteenth Edition. In one Volume. Cr. 8vo. Buckram, 7s. 6d. net.*

Belloc (H.)—
PARIS, 8s. 6d. net. HILLS AND THE SEA, 6s. net. ON NOTHING AND KINDRED SUBJECTS, 6s. net. ON EVERYTHING, 6s. net. ON SOMETHING, 6s. net. FIRST AND LAST, 6s. net. THIS AND THAT AND THE OTHER, 6s. net. MARIE ANTOINETTE, 18s. net. THE PYRENEES, 10s. 6d. net.

Bloemfontein (Bishop of). ARA CŒLI: AN ESSAY IN MYSTICAL THEOLOGY. *Seventh Edition. Cr. 8vo. 5s. net.* FAITH AND EXPERIENCE. *Third Edition. Cr. 8vo. 5s. net.* THE CULT OF THE PASSING MOMENT. *Fourth Edition. Cr. 8vo. 5s. net.* THE ENGLISH CHURCH AND RE-UNION. *Cr. 8vo. 5s. net.* SCALA MUNDI. *Cr. 8vo. 4s. 6d. net.*

Chesterton (G. K.)—
THE BALLAD OF THE WHITE HORSE. ALL THINGS CONSIDERED. TREMENDOUS TRIFLES. ALARMS AND DISCURSIONS. A MISCELLANY OF MEN. *All Fcap. 8vo. 6s. net.* WINE, WATER, AND SONG. *Fcap. 8vo. 1s. 6d. net.*

Hutton-Brock (A.). THOUGHTS ON THE WAR. *Ninth Edition. Fcap. 8vo. 1s. 6d. net.* WHAT IS THE KINGDOM OF HEAVEN? *Fourth Edition. Fcap. 8vo. 5s. net.* ESSAYS ON ART. *Second Edition. Fcap. 8vo. 5s. net.*

Cole (G. D. H.). SOCIAL THEORY. *Cr. 8vo. 5s. net.*

Conrad (Joseph). THE MIRROR OF THE SEA: Memories and Impressions. *Fourth Edition. Fcap. 8vo. 6s. net.*

Einstein (A.). RELATIVITY: THE SPECIAL AND THE GENERAL THEORY. Translated by ROBERT W. LAWSON. *Cr. 8vo. 5s. net.*

Fyleman (Rose.). FAIRIES AND CHIMNEYS. *Fcap. 8vo. Sixth Edition. 3s. 6d. net.* THE FAIRY GREEN. *Third Edition. Fcap. 8vo. 3s. 6d. net.*

Gibbins (H. de B.). INDUSTRY IN ENGLAND: HISTORICAL OUTLINES. With Maps and Plans. *Tenth Edition. Demy 8vo. 12s. 6d. net.* THE INDUSTRIAL HISTORY OF ENGLAND. With 5 Maps and a Plan. *Twenty-seventh Edition. Cr. 8vo. 5s.*

Gibbon (Edward). THE DECLINE AND FALL OF THE ROMAN EMPIRE. Edited, with Notes, Appendices, and Maps, by J. B. BURY. Illustrated. *Seven Volumes. Demy 8vo. Illustrated. Each 12s. 6d. net. Also in Seven Volumes. Cr. 8vo. Each 7s. 6d. net.*

Glover (T. R.). THE CONFLICT OF RELIGIONS IN THE EARLY ROMAN EMPIRE. *Eighth Edition. Demy 8vo. 10s. 6d. net.* POETS AND PURITANS. *Second Edition. Demy 8vo. 10s. 6d. net.* FROM PERICLES TO PHILIP. *Third Edition. Demy 8vo. 10s. 6d. net.* VIRGIL. *Fourth Edition. Demy 8vo. 10s. 6d. net.* THE CHRISTIAN TRADITION AND ITS VERIFICATION. (The Angus Lecture for 1912.) *Second Edition. Cr. 8vo. 6s. net.*

Grahame (Kenneth). THE WIND IN THE WILLOWS. *Tenth Edition. Cr. 8vo. 7s. 6d. net.*

Hall (H. R.). THE ANCIENT HISTORY OF THE NEAR EAST FROM THE EARLIEST TIMES TO THE BATTLE OF SALAMIS. Illustrated. *Fourth Edition. Demy 8vo. 16s. net.*

Hobson (J. A.). INTERNATIONAL TRADE: AN APPLICATION OF ECONOMIC THEORY. *Cr. 8vo. 5s. net.* PROBLEMS OF POVERTY: AN INQUIRY INTO THE INDUSTRIAL CONDITION OF THE POOR. *Eighth Edition. Cr. 8vo. 5s. net.* THE PROBLEM OF THE UNEMPLOYED: AN INQUIRY AND AN ECONOMIC POLICY. *Sixth Edition. Cr. 8vo. 5s. net.*

GOLD, PRICES AND WAGES : With an Examination of the Quantity Theory. *Second Edition. Cr. 8vo. 5s. net.*

TAXATION IN THE NEW STATE. *Cr. 8vo. 6s. net.*

Holdsworth (W. S.). A HISTORY OF ENGLISH LAW. *Vol. I., II., III., Each Second Edition. Demy 8vo. Each 15s. net.*

Inge (W. R.). CHRISTIAN MYSTICISM. (The Bampton Lectures of 1899.) *Fourth Edition. Cr. 8vo. 7s. 6d. net.*

Jenks (E.). AN OUTLINE OF ENGLISH LOCAL GOVERNMENT. *Fourth Edition.* Revised by R. C. K. Ensor. *Cr. 8vo. 5s. net.*

A SHORT HISTORY OF ENGLISH LAW: From the Earliest Times to the End of the Year 1911. *Second Edition, revised. Demy 8vo. 12s. 6d. net.*

Julian (Lady) of Norwich. REVELATIONS OF DIVINE LOVE. Edited by Grace Warrack. *Seventh Edition. Cr. 8vo. 5s. net.*

Keats (John). POEMS. Edited, with Introduction and Notes, by E. de Sélincourt. With a Frontispiece in Photogravure. *Third Edition. Demy 8vo. 10s. 6d. net.*

Kipling (Rudyard). BARRACK-ROOM BALLADS. *205th Thousand. Cr. 8vo. Buckram, 7s. 6d. net. Also Fcap. 8vo. Cloth, 6s. net; leather, 7s. 6d. net.*
Also a Service Edition. *Two Volumes. Square fcap. 8vo. Each 3s. net.*

THE SEVEN SEAS. *152nd Thousand. Cr. 8vo. Buckram, 7s. 6d. net. Also Fcap. 8vo. Cloth, 6s. net; leather, 7s. 6d. net.*
Also a Service Edition. *Two Volumes. Square fcap. 8vo. Each 3s. net.*

THE FIVE NATIONS. *126th Thousand. Cr. 8vo. Buckram, 7s. 6d. net. Also Fcap. 8vo. Cloth, 6s. net; leather, 7s. 6d. net.*
Also a Service Edition. *Two Volumes. Square fcap. 8vo. Each 3s. net.*

DEPARTMENTAL DITTIES. *94th Thousand. Cr. 8vo. Buckram, 7s. 6d. net. Also Fcap. 8vo. Cloth, 6s. net; leather, 7s. 6d. net.*
Also a Service Edition. *Two Volumes. Square fcap. 8vo. Each 3s. net.*

THE YEARS BETWEEN. *Cr. 8vo. Buckram, 7s. 6d. net. Also on thin paper. Fcap. 8vo. Blue cloth, 6s. net; Limp lambskin, 7s. 6d. net.*
Also a Service Edition. *Two Volumes. Square fcap. 8vo. Each 3s. net.*

HYMN BEFORE ACTION. Illuminated. *Fcap. 4to. 1s. 6d. net.*

RECESSIONAL. Illuminated. *Fcap. 4to. 1s. 6d. net.*

TWENTY POEMS FROM RUDYARD KIPLING. *360th Thousand. Fcap. 8vo. 1s. net.*

Lamb (Charles and Mary). THE COMPLETE WORKS. Edited by E. V. Lucas. *A New and Revised Edition in Six Volumes. With Frontispieces. Fcap. 8vo. Each 6s. net.*

The volumes are :—
I. Miscellaneous Prose. II. Elia and the Last Essay of Elia. III. Books for Children. IV. Plays and Poems. V. and VI. Letters.

Lankester (Sir Ray). SCIENCE FROM AN EASY CHAIR. Illustrated. *Thirteenth Edition. Cr. 8vo. 7s. 6d. net.*

SCIENCE FROM AN EASY CHAIR. Illustrated. *Second Series. Third Edition. Cr. 8vo. 7s. 6d. net.*

DIVERSIONS OF A NATURALIST. Illustrated. *Third Edition. Cr. 8vo. 7s. 6d. net.*

SECRETS OF EARTH AND SEA. *Cr. 8vo. 8s. 6d. net.*

Lodge (Sir Oliver). MAN AND THE UNIVERSE : A Study of the Influence of the Advance in Scientific Knowledge upon our Understanding of Christianity. *Ninth Edition. Crown 8vo. 7s. 6d. net.*

THE SURVIVAL OF MAN : A Study in Unrecognised Human Faculty. *Seventh Edition. Cr. 8vo. 7s. 6d. net.*

MODERN PROBLEMS. *Cr. 8vo. 7s. 6d. net.*

RAYMOND ; OR LIFE AND DEATH. Illustrated. *Twelfth Edition. Demy 8vo. 15s. net.*

THE WAR AND AFTER : Short Chapters on Subjects of Serious Practical Import for the Average Citizen in A.D. 1915 Onwards. *Eighth Edition. Fcap 8vo. 2s. net.*

Lucas (E. V.).
THE LIFE OF CHARLES LAMB, 2 vols., 21s. net. A WANDERER IN HOLLAND, 10s. 6d. net. A WANDERER IN LONDON, 10s. 6d. net. LONDON REVISITED, 10s. 6d. net. A WANDERER IN PARIS, 10s. 6d. net and 6s. net. A WANDERER IN FLORENCE, 10s. 6d. net. A WANDERER IN VENICE, 10s. 6d. net. THE OPEN ROAD: A Little Book for Wayfarers, 6s. 6d. net and 7s. 6d. net. THE FRIENDLY TOWN : A Little Book for the Urbane, 6s. net. FIRESIDE AND SUNSHINE, 6s. net. CHARACTER AND COMEDY, 6s. net. THE GENTLEST ART: A Choice of Letters by Entertaining Hands, 6s. 6d. net. THE SECOND POST, 6s. net. HER INFINITE VARIETY: A Feminine Portrait Gallery, 6s. net. GOOD COMPANY: A Rally of Men, 6s. net. ONE DAY AND ANOTHER, 6s. net. OLD LAMPS FOR NEW, 6s. net. LOITERER'S HARVEST, 6s. net. CLOUD AND SILVER, 6s. net. LISTENER'S LURE : An Oblique Narration, 6s. net. OVER BEMERTON'S : An Easy-Going Chronicle, 6s. net. MR. INGLESIDE, 6s. net. LONDON LAVENDER, 6s. net. LANDMARKS, 6s. net. A BOSWELL OF BAGHDAD, AND OTHER ESSAYS, 6s. net. 'TWIXT EAGLE AND DOVE, 6s. net. THE PHANTOM JOURNAL, AND OTHER ESSAYS AND DIVERSIONS, 6s. net. THE BRITISH SCHOOL: An Anecdotal Guide to the British Painters and Paintings in the National Gallery, 6s. net.

McDougall (William). AN INTRODUC-
TION TO SOCIAL PSYCHOLOGY.
Fourteenth Edition, Enlarged. Cr. 8vo.
7s. 6d. net.
BODY AND MIND: A HISTORY AND A
DEFENCE OF ANIMISM. *Fourth Edition.*
Demy 8vo. 12s. 6d. net.

Maeterlinck (Maurice)—

THE BLUE BIRD: A Fairy Play in Six Acts,
6s. net. MARY MAGDALENE; A Play in
Three Acts, *5s. net.* DEATH, *3s. 6d. net.*
OUR ETERNITY, *6s. net.* THE UNKNOWN
GUEST, *6s. net.* POEMS, *5s. net.* THE
WRACK OF THE STORM, *6s. net.* THE
MIRACLE OF ST. ANTHONY: A Play in One
Act, *3s. 6d. net.* THE BURGOMASTER OF
STILEMONDE: A Play in Three Acts, *5s.*
net. THE BETROTHAL; or, The Blue Bird
Chooses, *6s. net.* MOUNTAIN PATHS, *6s.*
net.

Milne (A. A.). THE DAY'S PLAY. THE
HOLIDAY ROUND. ONCE A WEEK. *All*
Cr. 8vo. 7s. net. NOT THAT IT MATTERS.
Fcap. 8vo. 6s. net.

Oxenham (John)—

BEES IN AMBER; A Little Book of Thought-
ful Verse. ALL'S WELL: A Collection of
War Poems. THE KING'S HIGH WAY. THE
VISION SPLENDID. THE FIERY CROSS.
HIGH ALTARS: The Record of a Visit to
the Battlefields of France and Flanders.
HEARTS COURAGEOUS. ALL CLEAR!
WINDS OF THE DAWN. *All Small Pott*
8vo. Paper, 1s. 3d. net; cloth boards, 2s.
net. GENTLEMEN—THE KING, *2s. net.*

Petrie (W. M. Flinders). A HISTORY
OF EGYPT. Illustrated. *Six Volumes.*
Cr. 8vo. Each 9s. net.
VOL. I. FROM THE 1ST TO THE XVITH
DYNASTY. *Ninth Edition. 10s. 6d. net.*
VOL. II. THE XVIITH AND XVIIITH
DYNASTIES. *Sixth Edition.*
VOL. III. XIXTH TO XXXTH DYNASTIES.
Second Edition.
VOL. IV. EGYPT UNDER THE PTOLEMAIC
DYNASTY. J. P. MAHAFFY. *Second Edition.*
VOL. V. EGYPT UNDER ROMAN RULE. J. G.
MILNE. *Second Edition.*
VOL. VI. EGYPT IN THE MIDDLE AGES.
STANLEY LANE POOLE. *Second Edition.*
SYRIA AND EGYPT, FROM THE TELL
EL AMARNA LETTERS. *Cr. 8vo.*
5s. net.
EGYPTIAN TALES. Translated from the
Papyri. First Series, ivth to xiith Dynasty.
Illustrated. *Third Edition. Cr. 8vo.*
5s. net.
EGYPTIAN TALES. Translated from the
Papyri. Second Series, xviiith to xixth
Dynasty. Illustrated. *Second Edition.*
Cr. 8vo. 5s. net.

Pollard (A. F.). A SHORT HISTORY
OF THE GREAT WAR. With 19 Maps.
Second Edition. Cr. 8vo. 10s. 6d. net.

Price (L. L.). A SHORT HISTORY OF
POLITICAL ECONOMY IN ENGLAND
FROM ADAM SMITH TO ARNOLD
TOYNBEE. *Ninth Edition. Cr. 8vo.*
5s. net.

Reid (G. Archdall). THE LAWS OF
HEREDITY. *Second Edition. Demy 8vo.*
£1 1s. net.

Robertson (C. Grant). SELECT STAT-
UTES, CASES, AND DOCUMENTS,
1660-1832. *Third Edition. Demy 8vo.*
15s. net.

Selous (Edmund). TOMMY SMITH'S
ANIMALS. Illustrated. *Eighteenth Edi-*
tion. Fcap. 8vo. 3s. 6d. net.
TOMMY SMITH'S OTHER ANIMALS.
Illustrated. *Eleventh Edition. Fcap. 8vo.*
3s. 6d. net.
TOMMY SMITH AT THE ZOO. Illus-
trated. *Fourth Edition. Fcap. 8vo.*
2s. 9d.
TOMMY SMITH AGAIN AT THE ZOO.
Illustrated. *Fcap. 8vo. 2s. 9d.*
JACK'S INSECTS. Illustrated. *Cr. 8vo. 6s.*
net.
JACK'S INSECTS. *Popular Edition. Vol.*
I. Cr. 8vo. 3s. 6d.

Shelley (Percy Bysshe). POEMS. With
an Introduction by A. CLUTTON-BROCK and
Notes by C. D. LOCOCK. *Two Volumes.*
Demy 8vo. £1 1s. net.

Smith (Adam). THE WEALTH OF
NATIONS. Edited by EDWIN CANNAN.
Two Volumes. Second Edition. Demy
8vo. £1 5s. net.

Stevenson (R. L.). THE LETTERS OF
ROBERT LOUIS STEVENSON. Edited
by Sir SIDNEY COLVIN. *A New Re-*
arranged Edition in four volumes. Fourth
Edition. Fcap. 8vo. Each 6s. net

Surtees (R. S.). HANDLEY CROSS.
Illustrated. *Ninth Edition. Fcap. 8vo.*
7s. 6d. net.
MR. SPONGE'S SPORTING TOUR.
Illustrated. *Fifth Edition. Fcap. 8vo.*
7s. 6d. net.
ASK MAMMA: OR, THE RICHEST
COMMONER IN ENGLAND. Illus-
trated. *Second Edition. Fcap. 8vo. 7s. 6d.*
net.
JORROCKS'S JAUNTS AND JOLLI-
TIES. Illustrated. *Seventh Edition.*
Fcap. 8vo. 6s. net.
MR. FACEY ROMFORD'S HOUNDS.
Illustrated. *Third Edition. Fcap. 8vo.*
7s. 6d. net.
HAWBUCK GRANGE; OR, THE SPORT-
ING ADVENTURES OF THOMAS
SCOTT, ESQ. Illustrated. *Fcap. 8vo.*
6s. net.
PLAIN OR RINGLETS? Illustrated.
Fcap. 8vo. 7s. 6d. net.
HILLINGDON HALL. With 12 Coloured
Plates by WILDRAKE, HEATH, and JELLI-
COE. *Fcap. 8vo. 7s. 6d. net.*

Tileston (Mary W.). DAILY STRENGTH FOR DAILY NEEDS. *Twenty-sixth Edition. Medium 16mo.* 3s. 6d. net.

Underhill (Evelyn). MYSTICISM. A Study in the Nature and Development of Man's Spiritual Consciousness. *Eighth Edition. Demy 8vo.* 15s. net.

Vardon (Harry). HOW TO PLAY GOLF. Illustrated. *Thirteenth Edition. Cr. 8vo.* 5s. net.

Waterhouse (Elizabeth). A LITTLE BOOK OF LIFE AND DEATH. *Twentieth Edition. Small Pott 8vo. Cloth,* 2s. 6d. net.

Wells (J.). A SHORT HISTORY OF ROME. *Seventeenth Edition.* With 3 Maps. *Cr. 8vo.* 6s.

Wilde (Oscar). THE WORKS OF OSCAR WILDE. *Fcap. 8vo. Each* 6s. 6d. net.
I. LORD ARTHUR SAVILE'S CRIME AND THE PORTRAIT OF MR. W. H. II. THE DUCHESS OF PADUA. III. POEMS. IV. LADY WINDERMERE'S FAN. V. A WOMAN OF NO IMPORTANCE. VI. AN IDEAL HUS-
BAND. VII. THE IMPORTANCE OF BEING EARNEST. VIII. A HOUSE OF POME-GRANATES. IX. INTENTIONS. X. DE PRO-FUNDIS AND PRISON LETTERS. XI. ESSAYS. XII. SALOMÉ, A FLORENTINE TRAGEDY, and LA SAINTE COURTISANE. XIII. A CRITIC IN PALL MALL. XIV. SELECTED PROSE OF OSCAR WILDE. XV. ART AND DECORATION.

A HOUSE OF POMEGRANATES. Illustrated. *Cr. 4to.* 21s. net.

Wood (Lieut. W. B.) and Edmonds (Col. J. E.). A HISTORY OF THE CIVIL WAR IN THE UNITED STATES (1861-65). With an Introduction by SPENSER WILKINSON. With 24 Maps and Plans. *Third Edition. Demy 8vo.* 15s. net.

Wordsworth (W.). POEMS. With an Introduction and Notes by NOWELL C. SMITH. *Three Volumes. Demy 8vo.* 18s. net.

Yeats (W. B.). A BOOK OF IRISH VERSE. *Fourth Edition. Cr. 8vo.* 7s. net.

PART II.—A SELECTION OF SERIES

Ancient Cities

General Editor, SIR B. C. A. WINDLE

Cr. 8vo. 6s. *net each volume*

With Illustrations by E. H. NEW, and other Artists

BRISTOL. CANTERBURY. CHESTER. DUBLIN. EDINBURGH. LINCOLN. SHREWSBURY. WELLS and GLASTONBURY.

The Antiquary's Books

General Editor, J. CHARLES COX

Demy 8vo. 10s. 6d. *net each volume*

With Numerous Illustrations

ANCIENT PAINTED GLASS IN ENGLAND. ARCHÆOLOGY AND FALSE ANTIQUITIES. THE BELLS OF ENGLAND. THE BRASSES OF ENGLAND. THE CASTLES AND WALLED TOWNS OF ENGLAND. CELTIC ART IN PAGAN AND CHRISTIAN TIMES. CHURCH-WARDENS' ACCOUNTS. THE DOMESDAY INQUEST. ENGLISH CHURCH FURNITURE. ENGLISH COSTUME. ENGLISH MONASTIC LIFE. ENGLISH SEALS. FOLK-LORE AS AN HISTORICAL SCIENCE. THE GILDS AND COMPANIES OF LONDON. THE HERMITS AND ANCHORITES OF ENGLAND. THE MANOR AND MANORIAL RECORDS. THE MEDIÆVAL HOSPITALS OF ENGLAND. OLD ENGLISH INSTRUMENTS OF MUSIC. OLD ENGLISH LIBRARIES. OLD SERVICE BOOKS OF THE ENGLISH CHURCH. PARISH LIFE IN MEDIÆVAL ENGLAND. THE PARISH REGISTERS OF ENGLAND. RE-MAINS OF THE PREHISTORIC AGE IN ENG-LAND. THE ROMAN ERA IN BRITAIN. ROMANO-BRITISH BUILDINGS AND EARTH-WORKS. THE ROYAL FORESTS OF ENG-LAND. THE SCHOOLS OF MEDIEVAL ENG-LAND. SHRINES OF BRITISH SAINTS.

The Arden Shakespeare

General Editor, R. H. CASE

Demy 8vo. 6s. net each volume

An edition of Shakespeare in Single Plays ; each edited with a full Introduction, Textual Notes, and a Commentary at the foot of the page.

Classics of Art

Edited by DR. J. H. W. LAING

With numerous Illustrations. Wide Royal 8vo

THE ART OF THE GREEKS, 15s. net. THE ART OF THE ROMANS, 16s. net. CHARDIN, 15s. net. DONATELLO, 16s. net. GEORGE ROMNEY, 15s. net. GHIRLANDAIO, 15s. net. LAWRENCE, 25s. net. MICHELANGELO, 15s. net. RAPHAEL, 15s. net. REMBRANDT'S ETCHINGS, Two Vols., 25s. net. TINTORETTO, 16s. net. TITIAN, 16s. net. TURNER'S SKETCHES AND DRAWINGS, 15s. net. VELAZQUEZ, 15s. net.

The 'Complete' Series

Fully Illustrated. Demy 8vo

THE COMPLETE AMATEUR BOXER, 10s. 6d. net. THE COMPLETE ASSOCIATION FOOTBALLER, 10s. 6d. net. THE COMPLETE ATHLETIC TRAINER, 10s. 6d. net. THE COMPLETE BILLIARD PLAYER, 12s. 6d. net. THE COMPLETE COOK, 10s. 6d. net. THE COMPLETE CRICKETER, 10s. 6d. net. THE COMPLETE FOXHUNTER, 16s. net. THE COMPLETE GOLFER, 12s. 6d. net. THE COMPLETE HOCKEY-PLAYER, 10s. 6d. net. THE COMPLETE HORSEMAN, 12s. 6d. net. THE COMPLETE JUJITSUAN, 5s. net. THE COMPLETE LAWN TENNIS PLAYER, 12s. 6d. net. THE COMPLETE MOTORIST, 10s. 6d. net. THE COMPLETE MOUNTAINEER, 16s. net. THE COMPLETE OARSMAN, 15s. net. THE COMPLETE PHOTOGRAPHER, 15s. net. THE COMPLETE RUGBY FOOTBALLER, ON THE NEW ZEALAND SYSTEM, 12s. 6d. net. THE COMPLETE SHOT, 16s. net. THE COMPLETE SWIMMER, 10s. 6d. net. THE COMPLETE YACHTSMAN, 16s. net.

The Connoisseur's Library

With numerous Illustrations. Wide Royal 8vo. 25s. net each volume

ENGLISH COLOURED BOOKS. ENGLISH FURNITURE. ETCHINGS. EUROPEAN ENAMELS. FINE BOOKS. GLASS. GOLDSMITHS' AND SILVERSMITHS' WORK. ILLUMINATED MANUSCRIPTS. IVORIES. JEWELLERY. MEZZOTINTS. MINIATURES. PORCELAIN. SEALS. WOOD SCULPTURE.

Handbooks of Theology

Demy 8vo

THE DOCTRINE OF THE INCARNATION, 15s. net. A HISTORY OF EARLY CHRISTIAN DOCTRINE, 16s. net. INTRODUCTION TO THE HISTORY OF RELIGION, 12s. 6d. net. AN INTRODUCTION TO THE HISTORY OF THE CREEDS, 12s. 6d. net. THE PHILOSOPHY OF RELIGION IN ENGLAND AND AMERICA, 12s. 6d. net. THE XXXIX ARTICLES OF THE CHURCH OF ENGLAND, 15s. net.

Health Series

Fcap. 8vo. 2s. 6d. net

THE BABY. THE CARE OF THE BODY. THE CARE OF THE TEETH. THE EYES OF OUR CHILDREN. HEALTH FOR THE MIDDLE-AGED. THE HEALTH OF A WOMAN. THE HEALTH OF THE SKIN. HOW TO LIVE LONG. THE PREVENTION OF THE COMMON COLD. STAYING THE PLAGUE. THROAT AND EAR TROUBLES. TUBERCULOSIS. THE HEALTH OF THE CHILD, 2s. net.

Leaders of Religion

Edited by H. C. BEECHING. *With Portraits*

Crown 8vo. 3s. net each volume

The Library of Devotion

Handy Editions of the great Devotional Books, well edited.
With Introductions and (where necessary) Notes

Small Pott 8vo, cloth, 3s. net and 3s. 6d. net

Little Books on Art

With many Illustrations. Demy 16mo. 5s. net each volume

Each volume consists of about 200 pages, and contains from 30 to 40 Illustrations, including a Frontispiece in Photogravure

ALBRECHT DÜRER. THE ARTS OF JAPAN. BOOKPLATES. BOTTICELLI. BURNE-JONES. CELLINI. CHRISTIAN SYMBOLISM. CHRIST IN ART. CLAUDE. CONSTABLE. COROT. EARLY ENGLISH WATER-COLOUR. ENAMELS. FREDERIC LEIGHTON. GEORGE ROMNEY GREEK ART. GREUZE AND BOUCHER. HOLBEIN. ILLUMINATED MANUSCRIPTS. JEWELLERY. JOHN HOPPNER. Sir JOSHUA REYNOLDS. MILLET. MINIATURES. OUR LADY IN ART. RAPHAEL. RODIN. TURNER. VANDYCK. VELAZQUEZ. WATTS.

The Little Guides

With many Illustrations by E. H. NEW and other artists, and from photographs

Small Pott 8vo. 4s. net and 6s. net

Guides to the English and Welsh Counties, and some well-known districts

The main features of these Guides are (1) a handy and charming form ; (2) illustrations from photographs and by well-known artists ; (3) good plans and maps ; (4) an adequate but compact presentation of everything that is interesting in the natural features, history, archæology, and architecture of the town or district treated.

The Little Quarto Shakespeare

Edited by W. J. CRAIG. With Introductions and Notes

*Pott 16mo. 40 Volumes. Leather, price 1s. 9d. net each volume
Cloth, 1s. 6d.*

Nine Plays

Fcap. 8vo. 3s. 6d. net

ACROSS THE BORDER. Beulah Marie Dix. *Cr. 8vo.*

HONEYMOON, THE. A Comedy in Three Acts. Arnold Bennett. *Third Edition.*

GREAT ADVENTURE, THE. A Play of Fancy in Four Acts. Arnold Bennett. *Fifth Edition.*

MILESTONES. Arnold Bennett and Edward Knoblock. *Ninth Edition.*

IDEAL HUSBAND, AN. Oscar Wilde. *Acting Edition.*

KISMET. Edward Knoblock. *Fourth Edition.*

TYPHOON. A Play in Four Acts. Melchior Lengyel. English Version by Laurence Irving. *Second Edition.*

WARE CASE, THE. George Pleydell.

GENERAL POST. J. E. Harold Terry. *Second Edition.*

Sports Series

Illustrated. Fcap. 8vo. 2s. net and 3s. net

ALL ABOUT FLYING, 3s. net. GOLF DO'S AND DONT'S. THE GOLFING SWING. HOW TO SWIM. LAWN TENNIS, 3s. net. SKAT-ING, 3s. net. CROSS-COUNTRY SKI-ING, 5s. net. WRESTLING, 2s. net. QUICK CUTS TO GOOD GOLF, 2s. 6d. net.

The Westminster Commentaries

General Editor, WALTER LOCK

Demy 8vo

THE ACTS OF THE APOSTLES, 16s. net. AMOS, 8s. 6d. net. I. CORINTHIANS, 8s. 6d. net. EXODUS, 15s. net. EZEKIEL, 12s. 6d. net. GENESIS, 16s. net. HEBREWS, 8s. 6d. net. ISAIAH, 16s. net. JEREMIAH, 16s. net. JOB, 8s. 6d. net. THE PASTORAL EPISTLES, 8s. 6d. net. THE PHILIPPIANS, 8s. 6d. net. ST. JAMES, 8s. 6d. net. ST. MATTHEW, 15s. net.

Methuen's Two-Shilling Library

Cheap Editions of many Popular Books

Fcap. 8vo

PART III.—A SELECTION OF WORKS OF FICTION

Bennett (Arnold)—

CLAYHANGER, 8s. net. HILDA LESSWAYS, 8s. 6d. net. THESE TWAIN. THE CARD. THE REGENT: A Five Towns Story of Adventure in London. THE PRICE OF LOVE. BURIED ALIVE. A MAN FROM THE NORTH. THE MATADOR OF THE FIVE TOWNS. WHOM GOD HATH JOINED. A GREAT MAN: A Frolic. *All 7s. 6d. net.*

Birmingham (George A.)—

SPANISH GOLD. THE SEARCH PARTY. LALAGE'S LOVERS. THE BAD TIMES. UP, THE REBELS. *All 7s. 6d. net.*

Burroughs (Edgar Rice)—

TARZAN OF THE APES, 6s. net. THE RETURN OF TARZAN, 6s. net. THE BEASTS OF TARZAN, 6s. net. THE SON OF TARZAN, 6s. net. JUNGLE TALES OF TARZAN, 6s. net. TARZAN AND THE JEWELS OF OPAR, 6s. net. TARZAN THE UNTAMED, 7s. 6d. net. A PRINCESS OF MARS, 6s. net. THE GODS OF MARS, 6s. net. THE WARLORD OF MARS, 6s. net.

Conrad (Joseph). A SET OF SIX. *Fourth Edition. Cr. 8vo. 7s. 6d. net.*

VICTORY: AN ISLAND TALE. *Sixth Edition. Cr. 8vo. 9s. net.*

Corelli (Marie)—

A ROMANCE OF TWO WORLDS, 7s. 6d. net. VENDETTA: or, The Story of One Forgotten, 8s. net. THELMA: A Norwegian Princess, 8s. 6d. net. ARDATH: The Story of a Dead Self, 7s. 6d. net. THE SOUL OF LILITH, 7s. 6d. net. WORMWOOD: A Drama of Paris, 8s. net. BARABBAS: A Dream of the World's Tragedy, 8s. net. THE SORROWS OF SATAN, 7s. 6d. net. THE MASTER-CHRISTIAN, 8s. 6d. net. TEMPORAL POWER: A Study in Supremacy, 6s. net. GOD'S GOOD MAN: A Simple Love Story, 8s. 6d. net. HOLY ORDERS: The Tragedy of a Quiet Life, 8s. 6d. net. THE MIGHTY ATOM, 7s. 6d. net. BOY: A Sketch, 7s. 6d. net CAMEOS, 6s. net. THE LIFE EVERLASTING, 8s. 6d. net.

Doyle (Sir A. Conan). ROUND THE RED LAMP. *Twelfth Edition. Cr. 8vo. 7s. 6d net.*

Hichens (Robert)—

TONGUES OF CONSCIENCE, 7s. 6d. net. FELIX: Three Years in a Life, 7s. 6d. net. THE WOMAN WITH THE FAN, 7s. 6d. net. BYEWAYS, 7s. 6d. net. THE GARDEN OF ALLAH, 8s. 6d. net. THE CALL OF THE BLOOD, 8s. 6d. net. BARBARY SHEEP, 6s. net. THE DWELLERS ON THE THRESHOLD, 7s. 6d. net. THE WAY OF AMBITION, 7s. 6d. net. IN THE WILDERNESS, 7s. 6d. net.

Hope (Anthony)—

A CHANGE OF AIR. A MAN OF MARK. THE CHRONICLES OF COUNT ANTONIO. SIMON DALE. THE KING'S MIRROR. QUISANTÉ. THE DOLLY DIALOGUES. TALES OF TWO PEOPLE. A SERVANT OF THE PUBLIC. MRS. MAXON PROTESTS. A YOUNG MAN'S YEAR. BEAUMAROY HOME FROM THE WARS. *All 7s. 6d. net.*

Jacobs (W. W.)—

MANY CARGOES, 5s. *net* and 2s. 6d. *net.* SEA URCHINS, 5s. *net* and 3s. 6d. *net.* A MASTER OF CRAFT, 5s. *net.* LIGHT FREIGHTS, 5s. *net.* THE SKIPPER'S WOOING, 5s. *net.* AT SUNWICH PORT, 5s. *net.* DIALSTONE LANE, 5s. *net.* ODD CRAFT, 5s. *net.* THE LADY OF THE BARGE, 5s. *net.* SALTHAVEN, 5s. *net.* SAILORS' KNOTS, 5s. *net.* SHORT CRUISES, 5s. *net.*

London (Jack). WHITE FANG. *Ninth Edition. Cr. 8vo. 7s. 6d. net.*

McKenna (Stephen)—

SONIA : Between Two Worlds, 8s. *net.* NINETY-SIX HOURS' LEAVE, 7s. 6d. *net.* THE SIXTH SENSE, 6s. *net.* MIDAS & SON, 8s. *net.*

Malet (Lucas)—

THE HISTORY OF SIR RICHARD CALMADY : A Romance. THE WAGES OF SIN. THE CARISSIMA. THE GATELESS BARRIER. DEADHAM HARD. *All 7s. 6d. net.*

Mason (A. E. W.). CLEMENTINA. Illustrated. *Ninth Edition. Cr. 8vo. 7s. 6d. net.*

Maxwell (W. B.)—

VIVIEN. THE GUARDED FLAME. ODD LENGTHS. HILL RISE. THE REST CURE. *All 7s. 6d. net.*

Oxenham (John)—

A WEAVER OF WEBS. PROFIT AND LOSS. THE SONG OF HYACINTH, and Other Stories. LAURISTONS. THE COIL OF CARNE. THE QUEST OF THE GOLDEN ROSE. MARY ALL-ALONE. BROKEN SHACKLES. "1914." *All 7s. 6d. net.*

Parker (Gilbert)—

PIERRE AND HIS PEOPLE. MRS. FALCHION. THE TRANSLATION OF A SAVAGE. WHEN VALMOND CAME TO PONTIAC : The Story of a Lost Napoleon. AN ADVENTURER OF THE NORTH : The Last Adventures of 'Pretty Pierre.' THE SEATS OF THE MIGHTY. THE BATTLE OF THE STRONG : A Romance of Two Kingdoms. THE POMP OF THE LAVILETTES. NORTHERN LIGHTS. *All 7s. 6d. net.*

Phillpotts (Eden)—

CHILDREN OF THE MIST. SONS OF THE MORNING. THE RIVER. THE AMERICAN PRISONER. DEMETER'S DAUGHTER. THE HUMAN BOY AND THE WAR. *All 7s. 6d. net.*

Ridge (W. Pett)—

A SON OF THE STATE, 7s. 6d. *net.* THE REMINGTON SENTENCE, 7s. 6d. *net.* MADAME PRINCE, 7s. 6d. *net.* TOP SPEED, 7s. 6d. *net.* SPECIAL PERFORMANCES, 6s. *net.* THE BUSTLING HOURS, 7s. 6d. *net.*

Rohmer (Sax)—

THE DEVIL DOCTOR. THE SI-FAN. MYSTERIES. TALES OF SECRET EGYPT. THE ORCHARD OF TEARS. THE GOLDEN SCORPION. *All 7s. 6d. net.*

Swinnerton (F.). SHOPS AND HOUSES. *Third Edition. Cr. 8vo. 7s. 6d. net.* SEPTEMBER. *Third Edition. Cr. 8vo. 7s. 6d. net.*

Wells (H. G.). BEALBY. *Fourth Edition. Cr. 8vo. 7s. 6d. net.*

Williamson (C. N. and A. M.)—

THE LIGHTNING CONDUCTOR : The Strange Adventures of a Motor Car. LADY BETTY ACROSS THE WATER. SCARLET RUNNER. LORD LOVELAND DISCOVERS AMERICA. THE GUESTS OF HERCULES. IT HAPPENED IN EGYPT. A SOLDIER OF THE LEGION. THE SHOP GIRL. THE LIGHTNING CONDUCTRESS. SECRET HISTORY. THE LOVE PIRATE. *All 7s. 6d. net.* CRUCIFIX CORNER. 6s. *net.*

Methuen's Two-Shilling Novels

Cheap Editions of many of the most Popular Novels of the day

Fcap. 8vo